Advance Praise

"Jennifer Wallig does a great job explaining how hard it can be to search for a birth family after a closed adoption. Her struggles and the emotions of the journey make you feel like you're by her side for the roller-coaster ride. She captures the emotions of first contact and how to be patient when developing a new relationship. Finding Max is a must-read, even if you're not in the adoption arena; it's about family and inspiration."

—MARIE ANDERSON, COORDINATOR FOR THE ADOPTEES' LIBERTY MOVEMENT ASSOCIATION (ALMA)

"Jennifer's account of Finding Max is an engaging story of the process and unintended discoveries of searching your ancestry, whether adopted or not. She shares her failures, vulnerabilities, surprises, and tenderness of the experience. Some of the moments are raw and hard, but others are profoundly moving, and give a renewed sense of faith in family."

—KATHLEEN NIELSEN, FORMER REGENT OF NSDAR, ANNE LOUCKS CHAPTER

"The path to discovering one's origin story is often filled with stop signs, potholes, and detours, and when that path is for a loved one, the challenges can become tenfold. Jennifer's chronicle of this journey, not only for herself but for her father, is enthralling and interesting as she walks you through her travails, revelations, and discoveries. If you have ever wondered what it is like to find your origin story, this is a read to include on your list!"

—GLENN MAU, PARTNER AT MOKRI VANIS & JONES, LLP

Finding Max

FINDING MAX

A Story *of* Family Secrets, Locked Doors, *and a* Journey *to* Uncover the Truth

JENNIFER WALLIG

COPYRIGHT © 2024 JENNIFER WALLIG
All rights reserved.

FINDING MAX
A Story of Family Secrets, Locked Doors, and a Journey to Uncover the Truth

FIRST EDITION

ISBN   978-1-5445-4728-2   *Hardcover*
         978-1-5445-4630-8   *Paperback*
         978-1-5445-4629-2   *Ebook*

for Dayo

CONTENTS

INTRODUCTION ... 11
1. GRANDMA GINI'S HOUSE ... 15
2. THE DISCOVERY ... 29
3. LOCKED DOORS ... 47
4. SISTERS AND LIES ... 67
5. THE TRUTH ... 83
6. ARE YOU SITTING DOWN? ... 93
7. A TRIP TO TEXAS ... 109
8. BROTHERS ... 125
9. CODA ... 135
10. CLOSURE ... 159
    EPILOGUE ... 169
    MISCELLANEOUS PHOTOGRAPHS ... 173
    ADDITIONAL RESOURCES ... 201
    ACKNOWLEDGMENTS ... 203
    ABOUT THE AUTHOR ... 205

INTRODUCTION

—

A YEAR OR SO AGO, AT A FAMILY REUNION, YOU GOT cornered by Great-Aunt Agatha.

Great-Aunt Agatha is chatty. *Very chatty*. But this particular afternoon, she also happened to be tipsy. You suspect your nephew of sneaking something in her lemonade, but that's beside the point, because, just as you're zoning out, doing your best to nod politely, you catch something interesting.

"And so, you see," she's saying, "my sister was actually married *before she met* Grandpa! And get this—*he was a carny*! How do you like them apples?" She laughs and pokes you in the arm.

Suddenly you're riveted and paying attention. "Really?" you ask.

"Yes, really. Ever wondered why your uncle Mark looks *nothing* like your grandpa? The freckles? The cleft chin? Not in this family, I tell you."

You try to get her to tell you more, but she just shakes her head and meanders over to the dessert table.

Intrigued by Great-Aunt Agatha's reveal, you spend the next few months trying to research your grandmother's first marriage.

But nothing really comes of it. Both of your grandparents have passed away, and Great-Aunt Agatha is back to being sober—and uninformative. And you don't know how you'd *possibly* broach the subject with Uncle Mark.

Nevertheless, something inside you longs to know the truth. You've always loved solving mysteries and puzzles, and you're deeply interested in ancestry and family genealogy. But what now? It feels like you keep hitting brick walls.

What you *really* need is some inspiration.

* * *

I grew up poor, on welfare, and in the low-income area of West Pittsburg. My parents divorced when I was about two, and for as long as I can remember, my dad was "a weekend dad." Living with my mom had its challenges too. We were forced to move frequently. I was always looking to the horizon and wanting more.

Both sets of my grandparents were actually upper-middle class. Go figure. When I would visit my grandmothers, I knew *this* was how I wanted to live. I wanted a nice house with a refrigerator—full of food! From an early age I focused on doing things to better my situation—from fundraising to simultaneously babysitting five kids for $1.50 an hour—so I could go to Fifth Grade Camp. From an early age, I was absolutely *determined* to solve situations and to go the extra mile to accomplish my dreams.

The story I'm about to share with you reflects that same resilience and dedication that I developed early on.

When I was a young teenager, I learned that my father was adopted. Suddenly—like in the story above, when Great-Aunt Agatha told you about her sister's first husband—a seed was planted in me. I longed to know more. Who were my dad's biological parents? What did this mean for our ancestry? Did we have any genetic disorders? Did I have another grandmother out there who was waiting and hoping that I'd find her? What if I found her and she didn't want to meet my dad—could we both handle the rejection?

And perhaps, most importantly, *where should I begin?*

My story spans thirty-five years—from 1989 to the present. As a teenager in a pre-internet era, I searched phone books and support groups and even placed ads in local newspapers. As more technology became available, I discovered family secrets and lies that led me astray in my research. As with so many journeys, nothing went as planned.

Part memoir, part practical advice for those looking for lost family and wanting to learn more about their genealogy, my goal in this book is to inspire others in their quest for truth. I will share with you tips and tricks I used to find information, including nonprofit societies and various other resources.

But make no mistake. This is *not* a research guidebook.

This is the story of my journey. And one I profoundly hope will inspire you in your genealogical pursuits.

This is a story about determination, heartache, slammed doors, brick walls, genealogy, DNA, and, ultimately, *family*. It is about the heart-warming, life-affirming joy that only a new family connection can bring. My story ends with a beautiful discovery, even if it wasn't the discovery I'd been searching for.

Come follow me down the rabbit hole and let me share with you the journey of finding Max. Because sometimes we don't know what we need until we find it.

Chapter 1

GRANDMA GINI'S HOUSE

IN MANY WAYS, IT WAS A TYPICAL SUNDAY AFTERNOON in 1989.

My dad, who had season tickets, was cheering on the 49ers at Candlestick Park, and I was having girl time with Grandma Gini at her beautiful house.

Perched atop a hill above the freeway and Walnut Creek neighborhood, her property held a beautiful view of Mount Diablo, which glowed green and gold during the day and pink and violet at sunset. The regular *whizz* of BART trains down below acted like comforting white noise. Walnuts and oaks peppered the land, filling the air with their dust of cracked nut shells and acorns. I always imagined that was how the Old West must have smelled. Bluebirds, drunk from the red berries of pyracantha bushes, swirled and dove among the fruits and vegetables in Grandma Gini's walled garden.

The house was a modest, long, single-story structure, painted olive green, as if to blend in with the surrounding hills. To a child, it felt massive, like a mansion. I loved exploring all through it, everytime it was my dad's weekend to keep me and I was able to be with Grandma Gini.

Inside, the house felt just as lush as the hill on which it sat. It was like stepping back into the coolest Victorian world that I could imagine. Tasteful lace doilies decorated beautifully oiled antique wooden tables. A shining white sofa with bright-gold-beaded pillows dominated the center of the living room.

And then, of course, there was Pearl. In front of the grand living room window, on a rocking chair between end tables and porcelain lamps, she sat: a legless, armless, female mannequin. While she may have been only a head and torso, Grandma Gini made sure Pearl matched the elegance of the room. She was done up like a 1960s secretary—tight black pencil skirt, white long-sleeved silk blouse, a tasteful string of pearls, flowing black hair, long eyelashes, and full makeup. Were it not for the blanket hiding her absent bottom half, she would have looked quite lifelike, and I expect she existed in that front window as an intruder deterrent. I absolutely loved her. She was like a giant Barbie doll, and I used to have conversations with her all the time.

I spent so many happy Sundays there.

We didn't really go on walks together because the terrain was so steep. And Grandma Gini wasn't one to take her grandchildren to parks or playgrounds. "I already raised my children," she'd say. So when we weren't hanging out at the house, we often ran errands together. Her father had been a jeweler, and she was in the family business as well. Their jewelry store, which was in the very ritzy Broadway Plaza, was one of my favorite places to visit. I don't know whether she took me there to show me off or whether she actually had business to conduct, but I loved the clean sparkle of the place. We also frequented Genova's Deli, which had (and still has!) the most perfect giant pickles. I'd snack on one while Grandma Gini did her shopping.

This particular afternoon, we were staying at her house. But something made *this* Sunday very different. If I could find the last-minute courage, I planned to drop a bomb on Grandma Gini.

For weeks, I'd been debating whether I should do it. The whole thing felt so...taboo. Maybe, I thought, families weren't supposed to talk about such things. When the time came, would I be brave enough to take a deep breath and *just ask*? Ever since my dad had dropped the bomb *on me* weeks before, I had been burning with hundreds of questions. But my dad seemed to lack not only answers but any curiosity on the subject as well.

Grandma Gini would have answers. She'd have to.

The one thing I never stopped to consider, though, was *how* to ask her. It was apparently beyond my sixteen-year-old comprehension to wonder how *the way* I asked her might draw a line between kindness and cruelty.

I was, after all, a teenager absorbed in my own complex world. I lived mostly with my mom, Jeanne, and stepdad, Vic, and they moved around all the time. Bouncing between crazy jobs with demanding overnight shifts or no work at all, they had fallen into a rhythm of skipping out on one landlord after another. My dad had fallen into his own rhythms of addiction and homelessness. (His beloved 49ers season tickets, which he never could have afforded, were a gift from Grandma Gini's partner, Lyle, who worked as a medical first aid supplier for the team.)

With so little support at home, high school remained a continual struggle for me. I seemed always on the verge of failing. On top of that, I was largely responsible for the well-being of my halfsister, Becky, who was ten years younger than me. The one bright spot in my life was my boyfriend, Joe, who I would eventually marry. Inspired by his work ethic and drive—and monumentally disappointed by my parents—I knew I wanted something more for my life. I knew *family* didn't have to be blown apart, unstable, and constantly on the move. I knew it had the potential to be life-giving.

But before I could even think about a better future, I needed to understand our family's past.

So there we were, Grandma Gini and I, on that typical Sunday afternoon. As we often did, we were snuggling on the white couch under a cozy white blanket, watching *The Golden Girls*. The show went to a commercial break, and I felt this was my chance.

I glanced over at Pearl. *Is this the moment, Pearl?* Afternoon sunlight danced on her black hair. I could see through her white silk sleeves where arms should have been. She smiled calmly back at me, unblinking. *Okay, Pearl. I hear you. It's now or never.*

"Hey, Grandma?"

"Mmm?"

"Dad recently told me he's—um—adopted." The last word rang through the air and I could feel it swirling and diving about the room like a bluebird.

We were shoulder to shoulder on the couch, and for a moment, Grandma Gini just stared ahead at the TV. A commercial for a new shade of Revlon lipstick, featuring Cindy Crawford, came on.

"Is that true?" I asked, worried maybe she—somehow—hadn't heard me.

Then, she shifted slightly on the couch so she could look at me. She drew in a slow breath. "Yes, that's true. He is." She studied my face for a moment. "Do you have any questions, honey?"

A few weeks earlier, when I'd last seen my dad, he had told me that he was adopted. It's funny how little I recall now of that particular conversation. I remember that it felt out of the blue and that it was clear he had no interest in continuing a conversation, saying something about how he didn't know anything else. I mostly remember that it felt *huge*. Grandma Gini wasn't his "real" mother? Or my "real" grandmother? What had happened? I burned to know everything. For weeks curiosity had churned inside of me. I couldn't ask my dad anything else. My mom wouldn't know. Grandma Gini was my only hope for relief.

And so, on that white couch in Grandma Gini's house, I finally found catharsis with her simple, but kind, opening: *Do you have any questions, honey?* I began to barrage her with questions.

"Why did you adopt him?"

"What about Uncle Steve? Is he adopted too?"

"Do you know anything about his real mom?"

"Did she ever try to get him back?"

Grandma Gini answered all my questions—but in that slightly vague, bits-and-pieces kind of way that parents do when they aren't yet ready to reveal everything to their child. Or, perhaps, when they're trying to disguise their own emotions. I learned that Grandma Gini and Don didn't think they could have their own children and so adopted my dad. Steve was their own biological child, who came later. She never met my dad's birth mom but knew she was an unwed teenager from San Jose, maybe a farmer's daughter. She was named Virginia, just like Grandma Gini. No, the birth mother had never tried to get him back.

I pushed on, hungry for more. "Does Uncle Steve know?"

"Yes," she answered patiently.

"Did he and Dad ever, like, have issues because of it?"

"No. Day and Steve are brothers."

"Do you—" I paused. The commercials had ended. Dorothy and Blanche were back to having some kind of argument. The audience burst out laughing when Dorothy gave her a withering look.

"Yes, honey? What is it?"

Do you love Steve more? That's what I wanted to ask. Because, *wouldn't she love him more?* Her own child who she'd carried inside her for nine months, who she'd wanted so much and for so many years that she'd settle for another woman's baby? Was my dad just a holding pattern until Steve came along? Had her love for Steve eclipsed the initial love she'd felt for my dad?

But I knew I couldn't. As much as I longed to know the truth, I also knew there was a line I couldn't cross. And maybe, just maybe, even in my sixteen year-old brain, a small part of me knew that it wasn't true—that it couldn't be true. As much as I feared she might have loved Steve more, perhaps I sensed a deeper truth. A child was a child. A mother was a mother.

It was time to stop asking questions.

"You know," said Grandma Gini, breaking the silence of my reflection, "if you ever want to ask anything else, you always can. Okay?"

I nodded. "Okay."

I don't know how Grandma Gini felt then, but I know she tried to answer me truthfully. Looking back I've often felt sadness that I bombarded her in this way. How painful to be asked about your son's "real" mom! Your son, who you loved more than anything in the world from the very first moment you first held him, who you raised, who you suffered over. *Of course she was his real mom*—not his birth mom, but his real mom nonetheless.

Despite the hurt I must have caused with my questions, Grandma Gini handled the situation with grace and poise. Just as she seemed to with everything in life. Who else but Grandma Gini could make a life-size mannequin with no arms or legs look elegant and perfectly at home? And who else could be blindsided by such a conversation and respond with patience and—there's no other word for it—generosity?

We went back to watching *The Golden Girls*.

* * *

When my dad dropped me off at my mom's later that afternoon, I ran to my bedroom. I had mentioned nothing of our conversation on the drive home. I needed to think about things on my own for a while. I quickly found a notebook and pen and wrote down everything Grandma Gini had told me. I didn't have a plan for what to actually *do* with the information. I just knew I needed to save it. Like a strange, powerful dream only just remembered on waking, I was afraid if I didn't capture her answers, they might just disappear. And I *really* didn't want this to disappear.

My family, until that afternoon at Grandma Gini's, had been so *un*mysterious. Disappointing, sure. Disjointed, sure. But not especially compelling—at least not to me. I may have had little direction at that point in my life, but I knew one thing: I didn't want to end up poor and constantly struggling like my mom and Vic or in and out of homelessness like my dad.

Even Grandma Gini, whom I adored, had her own messy story of a family. When my dad and Uncle Steve were still young, she and my grandfather, Don, divorced. He'd been a private contractor in Vietnam, and while I don't know exactly what happened, I expect it was the old story of the mother left at home with two young children, suspicions of a husband's infidelity, and a boatload of resentment. Not long after they divorced, Lyle came into the picture and stayed for more than twenty years until Grandma Gini left him for his best friend. Lyle, who was rude, outspoken, and brash, clashed with my dad, who was quickly turning into a bit of a screw-up. Constantly borrowing money and struggling with alcohol addiction, my dad seemed to piss Lyle off at every turn. Grandma Gini tried to help and console my dad as best she could, but a lot of damage had been done. It's funny, though, when Grandma Gini left Lyle for his sweeter, gentler best friend, it did something to humble Lyle. Later in life, he ended up a kind and loving old man. I grew up hearing terrible stories about him, but as an adult I took him shopping, brought him things, and very much enjoyed his company.

But on that Sunday afternoon, a new story about our family began to emerge. What that story was, exactly, I wasn't sure. But I felt I was on the cusp of something massive. And I wanted the truth.

Was it because I had little direction in my life and longed for something to propel me? I was always a resourceful child, and even from an early age I showed an entrepreneurial drive—a drive no doubt born out of my parents' constant money problems. When I wanted to be a cheerleader and they couldn't afford to buy the uniform, I'd just fundraise with chocolate bars or a math- or walk-a-thon. Or when I wanted to go to summer camp and they fought over whose turn it was to pay for it, I'd just say, *Screw it*, and I'd perform for some kind of door-to-door donations. When I wanted something, I always went after it.

Or was it because of all the romance books I'd been reading lately? You know, those Johanna Lindsey-type books, the ones in the grocery store checkout lines, with titles like *A Loving Scoundrel* or *Captive of My Dreams*. Their covers—dreamy, colorful scenes of bare-shouldered women caught up passionately in the arms of Fabio—transported me to other worlds. Worlds where a young Viking woman discovers long-buried family secrets and sets off on a great, romantic adventure. Worlds where a Regency woman, after one unexpected but feverish weekend with a pirate prince, is left with a secret child she can't possibly raise herself.

Probably, it was both. I'm tenacious and practical. But I'm also a romantic. I yearned to discover the truth of this new family story as much as I yearned to imagine it. What high seas adventure might this unburied family secret cast me into? And who was my father's father? A pirate prince, perchance?

But it would be another five years before I would do anything with the seeds of information Grandma Gini had given me. When I later rediscovered my notebook, it would set off an eighteen-year journey of research, filled with twists, turns, and dead end after dead end. Until, one day in 2009, I would make the startling discovery that would change my life—and my dad's—forever.

This is the story of that journey.

My great hope is that this story about perseverance and the heart-warming, life-affirming joy that only a new family connection can bring will inspire you to research your own family. Sometimes we don't know what we need until we discover it.

I have also made this a practical advice book for those looking for lost family and wanting to learn more about their genealogy. As such, at the end of each chapter, I include a section with lessons I learned along the way—and some I only learned in hindsight—in the hopes that they will help you too.

Grandma Gini, Don, and my dad at the Horner Family Cabin in Yosemite

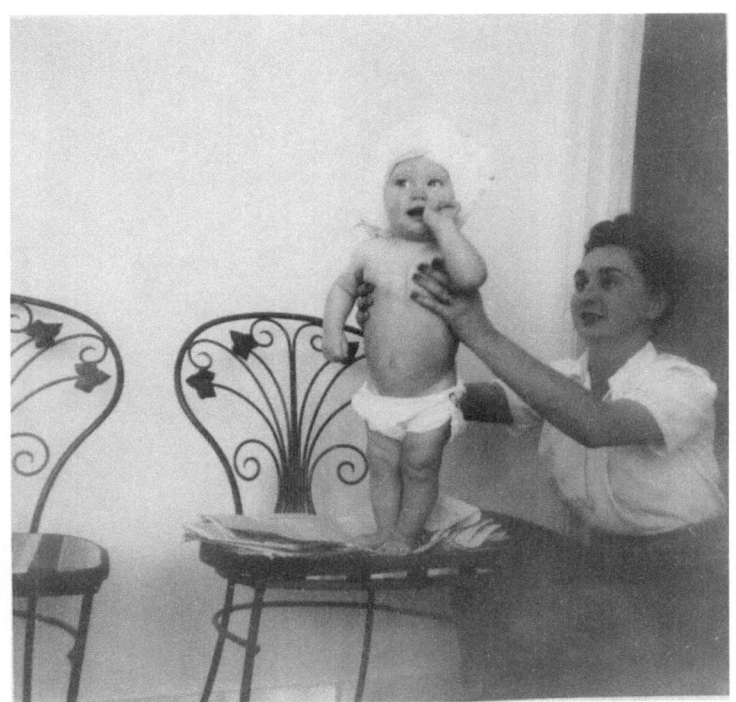

Grandma Gini and Dad, 1949–1950

Dad at a 49s game in 2015

A Pearl look-alike

KNOWING WHAT I KNOW NOW

If I could go back to that first conversation with Grandma Gini, I would approach it very differently. A lot just comes with age and maturity, of course, but when it comes to sensitive family conversations, particularly around adoption, I recommend the following:

1. Spend some time thinking through how you want to broach the subject. It's important to be prepared and not simply

speak off the cuff. You might even take notes on the questions you want to ask.
2. Spend some time thinking about the conversation from their perspective. What might their concerns be? What might hurt them? How can you approach the conversation with maximum empathy?
3. Don't just bust down the door. Give your family member a heads-up that you have some questions about X and would love to talk to them about it if they'd be comfortable.
4. If they don't want to talk, give them some space and time to sit with the idea before you approach it again.
5. If you're asking questions of an adoptive parent, give them assurance, if you can. For example, tell them they are a wonderful parent, that this isn't about trying to find someone who might have been better or more "real" than they are.
6. Take your cues from them. Don't ask rapid-fire questions, and listen more than you speak.

Chapter 2

THE DISCOVERY

I GRADUATED HIGH SCHOOL BY THE SKIN OF MY TEETH. For the next two years after my fateful conversation with Grandma Gini, I struggled just to get by when it came to schoolwork. But with my mom, dad, and Vic all wrapped up in their own troubles, no one was really parenting me. Despite knowing there would be no consequences, I dreaded the inevitable Ds and Fs that seemed blazoned across every report card. But then I'd get distracted by another social drama among my so-called friends and forget that I ought to stay on top of my assignments.

This cycle went on until the end of my junior year, when Joe began getting frustrated with me. He was already two years out of high school and out in the world doing his thing and succeeding.

"High school isn't a game," he'd say. "You *need* a diploma."

"I know, I know," I'd respond. But I never really made any changes.

But then he brought home for me what life would be like if I didn't graduate on time: I'd get stuck with the students in the year below me. My friends would graduate and move on without me. And—this was the kicker—if I didn't graduate on time, he'd break up with me.

Well, that did it. The importance of a diploma was vague and debatable—but the importance of Joe wasn't. Besides, the idea of being left behind—and left out—seemed terrifying at the age of seventeen!

I started taking classes at night and signed up for summer school. Over the next year I put my head down and worked my butt off.

My mom's jaw hit the floor when my first report card came back with all passing grades. "Why couldn't you have done this three years ago?"

I just rolled my eyes. Where had *she* been three years ago?

But—despite the odds against me—I did it. I graduated on time.

* * *

I mentioned my dad being wrapped up in his own troubles. The truth is, despite working for the carpenters union, he was homeless. He slept in his truck or couch surfed. Now and then, he'd find a cheap apartment or house to rent, but it never lasted for long. He lived from paycheck to paycheck, throwing most of it away on alcohol, marijuana, or amphetamines. It didn't help that many of the other carpenters he worked with were in similar boats.

At one point, when Dad was living in a friend's house in Antioch while commuting to Stockton for a job, he was in a drug deal gone wrong. Right as he was handing over cash to a new dealer, the dealer—and a couple of thugs—beat him up and took off with his payday cash.

Alone and bloodied, he somehow managed to make it back to his friend's house in Antioch. The next morning, a splitting headache and severe nausea worried him. But when he realized the dizziness was so bad he could barely stand and everything looked fuzzy, he called 911.

"I think I'm going to die," he told the operator before passing out and falling to the floor. He woke up in the hospital. Doctors had discovered a subdural hematoma and operated immediately to relieve the pressure on his brain. Left untreated, it would have killed him.

I didn't learn the truth of what had happened until a few weeks later, when he was about to be discharged.

"He'll stay with you, right?" I asked Grandma Gini. "While he recovers from the accident?" I knew he couldn't just go back to his truck or a couch in Antioch. He'd had major brain surgery!

"No, I can't allow that," she answered simply, coolly. She must have seen the confusion on my face because she then explained that it wasn't an accident and told me everything.

I was shocked. I knew he did some drugs, but I had no idea how bad it was. I guess you could say that I was the classic denial case. But if Grandma Gini wouldn't take care of him, I would.

My mom and Vic were currently renting a house that had an unused in-law unit in the backyard. I begged and begged my mom to let him stay there, assuring her he'd pay rent and stay out of trouble. After some serious consideration, and Vic's approval, she allowed it.

Dad living on the same property as me? Seeing him whenever I wanted, not just when he visited occasionally? I was ecstatic.

But my joy was short-lived. Once he recovered from the surgery, it wasn't long before he was back to drinking and getting high, and things soon turned sour between my parents. He was paranoid, thinking my mom was listening in on him and judging him. And it wasn't easy for Vic to have his wife's ex-husband around. So Dad moved out.

* * *

I soon began taking child development classes at a local junior college in Antioch. The combination of Joe's encouragement and my own realization that I *could* actually do well in school set a little fire under me. I was determined to complete my coursework, get my license to work in a daycare, take over the daycare as director, and then eventually own my own chain of daycares.

For the first time, my future looked exciting. I knew what I wanted. I had big dreams, and I was on my way to achieving them. I was unstoppable!

But then, just one year into child development classes, I had an epiphany. And an especially unfortunate one, given my new, big and shiny life plan. I hated children. The more I observed the chaos of nap times, snotty noses, and exploding diapers, the more I realized that working in a daycare (not to mention running a chain of them) would be my personal hell.

Suddenly, everything I thought I wanted disappeared. It was incredibly disheartening. What on earth would I do now?

I stopped taking classes and started working full time in retail at the mall. Meanwhile, I was still living at home with my mom and Vic, who moved constantly. And I was still taking on responsibilities for my younger sister, Becky. She was the cutest thing ever, but I was tired of having to be a responsible big sister. I was making so little money in retail that I couldn't afford to live on my own. I begged Joe, who was also still living with his parents, to move out with me. But he wouldn't because he knew we should save while we could.

I was bored and frustrated. This wasn't what my life was supposed to look like. I was desperate for an exciting change—something, anything to give my life direction and purpose.

Then, one day in 1993, I found it.

My mom and Vic were getting evicted from our house once again. We moved so much that I got to a point where I just stopped unpacking. Between kindergarten and fifth grade alone, we lived in five different places. And it felt like nearly every year after we moved again. I learned to keep unessential things from my childhood and teenage years taped up in cardboard boxes, which would leave one house and go to the next, untouched and unpacked.

But this time, for whatever reason, I decided to go through some of the boxes before we left. Maybe I didn't need to keep dragging those My Little Ponies, stacks of old magazines, and boxes of cassette tapes from my old Columbia House subscriptions around with me. In the bottom of one box, wedged beneath a bubblegum-pink Barbie bedroom set, was a thin stack of papers rubber banded together. Curious, I peeled off the rubber band and stared at my scrawl across one of the lined sheets.

The birth mother's name is Virginia.

She was seventeen.

She lived in a home for pregnant girls in San Jose.

My eyes nearly popped out of my head. So much had happened in the four years since my conversation with Grandma Gini. I'd failed class after class. I'd barely graduated high school. I'd started junior college and decided on a life path only to realize how wrong it was for me. I'd moved around countless times, and I'd started working full time. It wasn't that I forgot my father was adopted, but life's little dramas had intervened, making me forget how for one important Sunday three years earlier, I'd been completely absorbed in the mystery of his adoption. I recalled how I had run into my room after I got home, desperate to write down as much as I could remember.

I stared at my notes for the longest time. Turning them in my hands, reading and rereading what I'd written.

And then, just like that, for the first time in a long time, I felt a spark of excitement.

* * *

The next time my dad called, I was ready.

"Hey, Dad?" I jumped right in after we'd gotten through our initial check-ins. "I found those notes I took after Grandma Gini told me about your birth mom. I really want to dig into it all again. Would you be okay with that?"

There was a slight pause on the other end of the line. "Yeah, I'm fine with that. If that's something you want to do."

"I do! I really do. I don't know if I'm going to tell Grandma Gini or not because I don't want to hurt her feelings, but…I needed you to know."

But it was more than just needing him to know. I needed his outright permission. I wasn't sixteen anymore, and I understood that this wasn't *my* story. My history. Of course I wanted to know if I looked like my biological grandmother, but if I was going to start digging into the past, *his past*, I needed to know that I had his support.

My parents divorced when I was two, and Vic came into the picture two years later. He wasn't a bad stepfather, but he never really felt like a *father* to me. Sure, we had some good times together, but it wasn't until many years later that I realized he never actually loved me. I think Vic tolerated me because he wanted to be married to my mom, but that was just how it felt—

like I was being tolerated by this man who happened to be my mom's husband.

But from my own father, despite all his flaws and personal struggles, I always felt love. Even in these sporadic, long-distance phone calls, I could tell how he was feeling, and I knew he loved me like a father was supposed to love his daughter. And, unfortunately because of that, I was no stranger to getting him to do *exactly* what I wanted. I imagine this is somewhat common among children of divorced parents. I'm ashamed to admit it now, but I knew all the horrible plays. Throughout my childhood I played on both his guilt and his impotence as a father. You won't buy me an ice cream? You can forget that visitation next month! You're threatening to spank me? I'll never see you again! To this day, I feel guilty about these childish antics. Sometimes I think, *What a horrible daughter I was to a father who loved me, cherishing our weekend visitations.* I do recall later in adult life apologizing to him for some of my bratty behavior and thanking him for being such a cool dad.

So in many ways, I was used to my father telling me what I wanted to hear. I desperately wanted him to give me permission to research his birth mother. But I could tell he meant what he had said. He wasn't just trying to please me. I had his blessing.

"Jennifer?" he added as we were wrapping up the phone call.

"Yeah?"

"Just remember, even if you do find this woman—Grandma Gini is my mother."

* * *

My dad's permission fanned my spark of excitement. It grew into a fiery *need* to solve the mystery. I don't think I'd ever felt such a powerful drive within myself before.

I studied my sparse notes over and over. But what could I do with so little information? A first name? A city? It was 1993. I wouldn't even hear the word "internet" for a few more years.

I hesitated to ask Grandma Gini anything else. Would it hurt her? Did she even *know* anything else?

Soon enough, though, my burning curiosity won out. Besides, I was older now and understood better ways to approach the conversation.

Within the week, I drove to Grandma Gini's house. This time, there was no snuggling on the couch under a white blanket. There was no *Golden Girls* on the TV. Pearl still oversaw our conversation, but—maybe it was my imagination—she seemed a little tired, a little older this time.

Grandma Gini and I simply drank tea in the living room and talked about our lives. We talked about Becky, whom she loved, and my mom and Vic. We talked about Dad.

When the time seemed right, I brought it up.

"Do you remember years ago when I asked you about Dad's adoption?"

Grandma Gini looked up immediately from her tea. She seemed a little taken aback. Not angry or sad, just surprised.

I pushed on, gently. "Do you think I could…would it be okay if I asked you more about it?"

I expected her to sigh and say, "Sure, honey," while thinking, *Here comes the nosy granddaughter again. Why can't she just let sleeping dogs lie?*

But instead she put down her tea and stood up. Now I was the one who was surprised. *This* I hadn't expected.

"Hold on," she said and abruptly left the room. I stayed seated and nervously watched the hallway into which she'd disappeared. A minute or so later, she returned, carrying a small bundle of envelopes and papers.

"Here," she said, handing me the bundle. "This is everything I have." Her tone wasn't rude, but it *was* crystal clear: any answer she might be able to give me would be in that stack.

"Oh, okay. Wow. Thank you." I look down briefly at the stack of mostly lined papers and envelopes. I was dying to pounce on the whole stack and immediately start scouring it, but I stopped myself. I didn't want to offend her.

"I tried to give this to your dad years ago, but he wasn't interested."

I looked up. "I actually asked him about it this week," I replied. "I wanted to make sure it was okay with him if I pursued it further." I felt the weight of the treasure trove in my hands and smoothed one corner of an envelope that had been bent. "Are you okay if I try to find her?"

"Of course, honey. Day is a grown man, and I'm done with raising him. And look at you now! You're about to be a grown woman." She smiled at me.

Was it a real smile?

Or was it just punctuation, a shut-up-and-stop-asking-questions, full-stop period? I'm not sure now. I can't even imagine being in her position. She had survived raising her adopted son, who never wanted to know anything. He was content with her as his only mother. She'd never had to deal with it. And then *I* suddenly come along and surprise-bomb her life with wanting to dredge up the past.

The conversation soon turned to her house, which she was getting ready to sell so she could move to Citrus Heights. Grandma Gini and Lyle, her partner of nearly thirty years, had broken up. Lyle was rude and verbally abusive and, honestly, just kind of an all-around jerk. If Lyle was like *All in the Family*'s Archie Bunker, then Grandma Gini was a little bit like Edith in how she accommodated him. As a child, I never liked him.

Grandma Gini was leaving Lyle for his best friend, Dick. She and I never talked about her relationships or romances, so I can only guess why she made this move so late in life. Dick's wife had died a year or so before, so I assume Grandma Gini and Lyle started hanging out with Dick more and that a spark must have emerged between the widower and an unhappy Grandma Gini. Dick was a very gentle old man, well established, with a great background, and I can see why she would prefer to live out the rest of her days with someone who wasn't going to be a grumpy old jerk like Lyle. (Interestingly enough, in later years, Lyle turned into a whole new man. It seemed like his break up with Grandma Gini shook up his life and transformed him into a likable, actually enjoyable person to be around. I called him Grandpa Lyle in those later years.)

But that was it. That was the last time we ever spoke about Dad's adoption.

* * *

In the car, I kept looking over at the stack, which I'd placed gingerly on the passenger's seat. More than once, I nearly pulled over so I could start reading. It's just dumb luck I didn't get caught for speeding before arriving at home.

The stack, as it turned out, only contained one legal document, my dad's birth certificate, which falsely declared that Don and Virginia Horner were the birth parents of Dayton Louis Horner. Mostly, though, I found several handwritten notes in Grandma Gini's hand. It appeared to be everything she knew before adopting my dad: the hospital he was born in, the name of the doctors, the adoptive caseworker's name and case number. And his mother's name: Virginia Whitley. I didn't know it then, but *this was amazing information* for an adoptee to have! I had no idea how fortunate I was.

There was also a small series of letters between Grandma Gini and Virginia Whitley following the adoption. Amazingly, Grandma Gini had made handwritten copies of the letters she'd sent Virginia, so I was able to read their full correspondence.

1441 Ellis Street — Room 610
San Francisco, Calif.
November 30, 1948

Dear Mr. and Mrs. Horner:

    I imagine you are surprised to hear from me, but I have not heard anything concerning this matter for a long time, and perhaps you could write me some valuable information.

    I guess you realize that Mrs. Burrington turned the case over to Mrs. Van Colin, the <u>Head</u> lady in San Francisco. Mrs. Van Colin informed me not to rush into matters at all, because she said they did not advise putting babies into homes where the couples had only been married a short time. She said they would have an inspector come to your house, and check on everything. Have they done that? Furthermore she informed me <u>not</u> to sign <u>any</u> papers at least before Feb 1949. She stated that would give me plenty of time for more decisions. The <u>only</u> papers I signed, were in case of illness, giving my permission for medical care, or operations if needed! I was in a tight spot at that time and I was certainly happy you could keep him for me. Mrs. Buffington told me how happy you were!

    But — <u>if</u> I go ahead and sign papers later, I still would like a picture of you <u>3</u> this Xmas!

    Mrs. Van Colin also told me that if I paid you a reasonable monthly sum for his care and all the expenses, you would release him back to me. (This is what my father wants me to do) — But I realize

— 1 —

your side of the side too, so, I would appreciate a reply from you! Also, what you have done towards the line of adoption. I will expect a letter from you direct and a picture also.

Do you attend any church?

If so, which one? You folks have certainly been wonderful to do this for me, and I <u>assure</u> you, I <u>won't</u> be bother you, only I would appreciate a picture (3) of you and a letter <u>soon</u>.

Thanking you for your immediate attention to this letter, I am,

     Very truly yours,
     Virginia Whitley
     1441 Ellis Street, Room 610
     c/o G.T. College
     San Francisco, Calif.

P.S. Mrs. Van Colin gave me your address, and all information — about your status (Virginia Bower) etc. So don't feel that you are holding anything from me, but let's be good friends!

Did you name him Dayton Louis?
 —Write soon

Virginia Whitley's letter to the Horners

a copy of my reply to the letter

December 4th 1948

Dear Miss Whitley -

    I rather imagine that you have been anxious to hear about the baby and when we have been in San Jose, I did take the baby to see Mrs. Buffington so that she might tell you of his progress, as we had previously agreed, and I had hoped she would tell you how darling he is. We are of course completely devoted to the baby and he has brought so much happiness to our home.

    As to details about him, as I think you will enjoy them. He now weighs 18 pounds and is about 28 inches long. His coloring is very fair with the bluest of eyes, which, incidentally, match that of Mr. Horner, and as he is now almost eight months, he is sitting by himself and occasionally crawls an inch or two. You asked about his name and we did name him Dayton Louis, after his grandfather.

    By now you possibly know that the welfare lady, Mrs. York has called on us and so far as we do know has found all the necessary details in order and we have of course taken all the necessary legal steps that were required of us in the adoption of the baby. And naturally, will be happy when the final papers are signed and in order. Mr. Horner and I have wondered if it would ease your mind if you were to meet us. I certainly will be happy to do so if you should like. Or try to make some convenient arrangement for you.

    As to religion we are both Presbyterian and do attend church when its convenient now, but most of our days are the baby's at present until he's older and I do want you to know that we have given him every possible care known and our full love and affection.

    Virginia Horner

Grandma Gini's letter to Virginia Whitley

I found a fresh notebook in my room and wrote at the top of the first page: *Clues*. I copied everything from the letters and notes that seemed useful, and I also started a list of questions I'd need to follow up on. For as many questions as Grandma Gini's stack answered, it asked even more. Where was Virginia Whitley now? Did she still live at the return address in San Francisco? Had she married the father? Had she been pining all these years to know where her son was?

At the end of the last letter from Virginia Whitley, she mentioned Baby Gary. She seemed a little sad that they'd named him Dayton. There was a wistfulness in the letter, as if she might want her Baby Gary back. Was this the final letter because Grandma Gini sensed this potential threat to her new happy family life and ended their correspondence? Did Virginia Whitley write more letters, which Grandma Gini threw out? My romantic imagination played out several different scenarios. But in all likelihood, the correspondence simply came to a natural conclusion. After all, both women would want to get on with their lives, right? It impressed me, though, that Grandma Gini had kept the lines of communication open as long as she had. To me, it showed a good-faith effort to honor Virginia Whitley and what she'd given up.

Virginia Whitley's envelope with return address

Virginia Whitley of 1441 Ellis Street, San Francisco: here I come! Sure, it had been forty-five years, but I finally had a full name and address. I was going to find her.

I felt invincible.

KNOWING WHAT I KNOW NOW

Before beginning my research, I asked permission from both my father and my grandmother. I was lucky that I had not only their blessing but also my first real primary documents.

But what if I hadn't had outright permission? What if my dad had simply said, "No. I don't want you to do that." In all honesty, I would have pursued it secretly anyway. I was too gung ho to be stopped. I was so gung ho, in fact, that I hadn't stopped to consider that my life wouldn't just pause for my research. Over the next several years, my career and family would take precedence—as they should. Even if you're desperate to solve a mystery, you have to live your life first and all that comes with it.

If it was today, and my dad or Grandma Gini refused me permission, I would honor that refusal. I would respect the adoptee's wishes.

You must, of course, honor your own conscience. But know this: when you start researching family genealogy and adoptive history, you'll be digging into a past that a person may have forgotten or may not have ever known. You never know what you might discover. Some closets have pretty big skeletons! But even seemingly innocuous events can nevertheless have a big impact.

For example, I was recently researching some family history for a friend. I came across a newspaper article showing that she'd been in a bad car accident when she was three years old. My friend had no idea and was blown away. Why didn't she remember this? Had her parents kept it from her? If so, why?

Having respect for the wishes of others is really important. It's not all about your need to solve a puzzle. Whether young or old, it's easy to become absorbed in our own desires and not see how our choices affect those around us. *Try* to consider all possible outcomes to your research; ask yourself, "What if..." and then decide if you should pursue it. My husband always says, "Just because *you can* doesn't mean *you should*!"

For example, take my stepdad, Vic. His mother had a relationship with a married man and became pregnant with Vic. The man, of course, ditched Vic's mother in Oklahoma and moved to California. After having Vic, his mother decided to chase the man to California, where she lived within one county of him and eventually married a man named Torres. Much later in life, my stepsister, Alisha, Vic's daughter from his first marriage, did a DNA test and connected with Vic's biological half-siblings. Although his history was well known within our family, his siblings had no idea. At that point, their grandmother, Opal, who had been married to Vic's biological father, the one his mother had had the affair with, was ninety years old. Her children decided not to spring it on her that her husband had cheated on her all those years ago and had a child out of it. What good would that do?

Chapter 3

LOCKED DOORS

—

MY MOTHER, OF ALL PEOPLE, FOUND MY FIRST resource.

"They're called the Alma Society," she said one morning, thunking a phone book down on the breakfast table in front of me.

Remember when phone books were our go-to for everything? Once a year, they'd arrive on our doorstep, wrapped in that thin, clear, plastic bag. And they seemed to have everything! It's actually pretty amazing when you think about it. Fewer and fewer families keep a landline nowadays, and since emails and cell phone numbers are private, we no longer have a general directory for how to contact every person and every business in town.

"Adoptee Liberty something...hold on. Let me double-check." My mom leaned over the massive book, open to the Yellow Pages, and squinted. "Okay, there it is. Adoptees Liberty Movement Association. Alma."

I glanced up at her from my Cheerios, intrigued. She had a look of triumph on her face. "Thanks, Mom. Do you know what they do?" I asked, taking another bite of cereal.

"Sounds like they have workshops and things to help people find their families. I thought you and your dad could check them out."

That afternoon, when I got home from my job at the mall, I gave the Alma Society a call at their San Francisco Bay Area chapter.

Founded in 1971 by Florence Fisher, herself an adoptee, the Alma Society was a pioneer in helping adoptees fight for their rights. As it turned out, they not only sponsored workshops and support groups, but they also had an extensive registry to help adoptees, adoptive families, and birth families find and connect with each other. It was run entirely by volunteers.

I spoke with a woman named Claudia on the phone. She could not have been nicer. I told her what I knew and that I wanted to find Virginia Whitley but I wasn't sure where to start.

She explained that she would send me paperwork to provide Alma with any information I had about his adoption. Once the info was in the registry, it would allow for anyone who might be looking for us to find us.

Had Virginia Whitley been looking for her son all these years? The idea thrilled me.

Claudia recommended that Dad and I attend one of their workshops to learn more about the search process. "Our volunteers here will support your search in any way we can—legal, logistical, moral, whatever you need."

She also suggested that I reach out to a local organization, PACER (Post-Adoption Center for Education and Research), which was located in Orinda, California.

"You know, I hate to tell you this, Jennifer," she said as we were wrapping things up on the phone, "but California has closed adoptions. That means it's one of the hardest states in the country to find families."

> California now leans more toward an open adoption, but back then they weren't common. A closed adoption means the birth mother does not meet the adopting parents before or after the birth. She hands over the baby and signs the paperwork. This is the kind of adoption my dad had. The two parties never met face to face. An open adoption is when there is communication and possible meetings before and after the birth. This keeps the lines of communication open and an opportunity for the adoptee to learn their heritage should they want to learn more.
>
> Alabama, Alaska, Connecticut, Colorado, Kansas, Louisiana, Maine, Massachusetts, New Hampshire, New York, Oregon, Rhode Island, South Dakota, and Vermont are the only US states where adult adoptees have unrestricted access to their own original birth records!

My heart sank. I was just getting started on my research. One of the hardest states?

"And also, you know," Claudia added, "adoption laws were different in the 1940s." She explained that back in those days, closed adoptions were more common. Not so much for the welfare of the child but to protect the adoptive parents from interference from the birth family coming to try to take the baby back or intrude on the new family. So records like my dad's were "sealed."

When I received the paperwork from Claudia in the mail, I filled it out with everything I knew about Dad's adoption and mailed it back. Now, if Virginia Whitley—or anyone else in her family—was looking for Dad, they'd be able to find him.

You'd think, given my eagerness to find Virginia Whitley, that I would have attended a workshop or immediately called up PACER. But I didn't. Dad still wasn't particularly interested in pursuing it himself, and life's distractions—nothing special, but distractions nonetheless—once again slowed down my search.

> In June 2023, the Alma Society ("dedicated to reuniting members of the adoption triad") closed their registration to new members. They have, however, continued to make their registry available to current members and maintained a Facebook page so those members can connect online. You can email them too: almasociety1971@gmail.com.

It was a year before I finally called the Post-Adoption Center for Education and Research (PACER). They were a nonprofit, staffed only by volunteers, and held separate monthly gatherings for adoptees and adoptive parents. I spoke with someone named Lee, who, like Claudia at the Alma Society, was very helpful. She told me about various nearby societies and agencies and shared tips and tricks for my search. She said she would send me their newsletter and said I should check out the International Soundex Reunion Registry (ISRR). And, if I could afford it, the Independent Search Consultants and States of Expertise could be another route I could take. But of course I couldn't afford it.

"You're lucky you know his birth name," Lee told me. "So many people don't."

A last, a glimmer of hope!

* * *

In 1994 I landed a job as a debt collector for a collection agency, which I thought would be a step up from the odd nannying or retail job I had. But the lack of a professional environment disappointed me. Imagine a giant room full of cubicles. Everyone was dressed in jeans and t-shirts, leaning back in their chairs, talking loudly on their phones and just tapping their pencils, staring blankly at their monitors. It wasn't my imagined hell of a career in daycare, which I'd decided against, but it was far from what I wanted. I'd been poor for so long, and inconstancy had been the only constant in my life so far. I longed for something better.

A few times I'd walked through our company's front office. It was beautifully structured and decorated. The clean carpets, the attractive art on the walls, the relative quiet of the space. The skirts and nylons, slacks and button-downs. Everyone busy and focused on their work. *This* was what a career was supposed to look like. I fell in love with all of it.

So one day I told my boss that they needed me up there, that I was meant to be in the front office with the secretaries and accountants and legal team—not back with the debt collectors—and that I would make their life easier.

I must have said something to make them trust me because I was soon promoted to a receptionist. And not long after that, I joined the legal team, where I stayed for four years. I was great in an office. I loved dressing up for work, keeping my desk organized, and solving problems efficiently. I felt prestigious and professional.

Finally, I had arrived.

* * *

My dad would soon arrive in his life too. But not before things got much worse.

One day, Dad called to tell me he wouldn't be able to visit that weekend. He was framing houses in Mammoth Lake, and the job was so big he wouldn't be able to get away. I was disappointed, of course, but this happened occasionally. I told him I understood and I'd see him next month.

Soon, though, I received an envelope in the mail with no return address. Inside was a newspaper clipping. *Huh?* I thought, and I began to read.

Two weeks prior, some crazy drunk named Dayton Horner had tried to run a poor couple off the road. In trying to pass them in a road rage, he'd swerved too hard and ended up rolling his car down the embankment, stopping only when his car had flipped and then wrapped itself around a tree below. Extricated by the jaws of life, Horner was now in jail for thirty days because he couldn't make bail.

The shock of that moment was unlike anything I'd ever experienced. I stared at the clipping before me. I was absolutely heartbroken. *How could he lie to me?*

When I showed the clipping to my mom, she replied, "Your dad's an alcoholic."

Those simple words slapped me in the face. I'd been in denial my whole life. *My father was an addict. An alcoholic.* What had I done? I'd just buried my head in the sand. But now he'd almost killed himself—not to mention two innocent people. The truth of his situation turned my heartbreak into fury. *How dare he?*

When he called me again a few days later from jail, I let him have it. I told him I never wanted to see him again and he was a liar and a jerk and every terrible insult I could summon.

That phone call may have been cathartic for me, but it was a turning point for Dad. When he got out of jail, he asked Grandma Gini and Dick for help. For real this time.

He was ready for rehab and asked if they would front the money for his recovery. Grandma Gini might not have wanted him convalescing in her home after he got jumped, but she was willing to pay for him to get help from professionals. So in May 1995, he checked into the Progress House for Men in Coloma. They received funding from Veterans Affairs and assigned Dad a case manager. Grandma Gini and Dick agreed to pay for his first few months there.

One year later, he was still living there and—most importantly—still sober. For the first time in his life, he'd begun to comprehend and deal with his mental health issues. He received intensive treatment for his now-diagnosed PTSD from having seen combat in Vietnam.

I'm also glad to say I was able to put my hurt and anger away, and I visited him there whenever I could. He became a version of my dad I'd only seen glimmers of before. I was so proud of him and encouraged him every way I could.

One year was a *huge* accomplishment. To commemorate his sobriety, he changed his license plate to read MAY 1995. He'd never need to change that plate. He'd be clean and sober for the rest of his life.

* * *

Not long after I landed in the legal team job, I went to visit Grandma Gini. I was eager to tell her how my new career was going.

She had moved to Citrus Heights and was living with Dick, but she still had the white sofa we'd spent so many hours on together. Pearl—no longer greeting guests or frightening away intruders—was perched in a guestroom chair by a window and Murphy bed. I missed the feeling of her quietly, elegantly participating in our conversations.

I immediately noticed Grandma Gini's hair was thinning. And underneath, something was clearly wrong with her scalp. It startled me. She always looked so healthy and put-together. But her scalp looked red now, almost bright red, as if it were on fire.

"Grandma, is your scalp okay? It looks pretty, um, irritated?"

She just waved her hand, as if to flick aside my concerns. "Oh, that just happens when you get older, honey."

But I wondered. She also seemed overly loving toward me. She'd always been affectionate, but this visit felt different. She kept touching me—stroking my hair or placing her hand on my hand. I didn't mind or think too much of it. I was just so happy to be in her company. We parted with our usual hug, "I love you," and "See you soon."

* * *

A couple of weeks later my phone rang, waking me up at six o'clock in the morning. I was still living at my mom and Vic's house, but I had my own phone line in my bedroom by then. No good news comes at that time of day.

"Jennifer?" It was Dick.

"Hi, Dick." I was groggy and confused. *Why was he calling me?*

"Your Grandma Gini passed away."

"What?" I gripped the phone tighter and sat up in bed. "What are you talking about?"

"It was cancer."

I tried to process his words. "I didn't even know she was sick."

"She had cancer."

"Oh." I thought back to the last time I'd see her, the thinning hair, the flame-red scalp. Was that from chemo? It must have been. Why hadn't she said anything? Was it a stiff-upper-lip thing? A Greatest Generation thing? Was that why she'd been so lovey dovey, why she'd hugged me so tightly? My breath caught in my throat.

"Jennifer?" Dick asked. "Will you please tell your dad for me?"

"Yeah, sure," I choked out. We hung up. A wave of disbelief and sorrow broke over me. I fell back onto the bed and sobbed.

When I finally wore myself out, I called the Progress House to leave a message for my dad. The residents didn't have individual lines. I just told them that we had a family emergency and he needed to call me back.

While I waited for his call, I paced my room. And I started to feel angry. Dick should have been calling my dad, not me. I was the granddaughter. How was I supposed to tell my dad that his mother was dead? Did he know anything about her cancer, or would this be a complete shock for him too? I knew things had been tense for a long time between Dick and Dad. Dick, like Lyle, always saw Dad as the screw-up, the addict. Dad had made so many mistakes for so many years that even one year's worth of sobriety wasn't enough to convince Dick that he was a changed man. I'm sure his skepticism affected Grandma Gini as well. But he *was* a changed man. That one year of sobriety would, one day at a time, turn into a lifetime of it. After that last drink a year earlier, he would never have another one. He'd eventually become a leader in the recovery community.

Despite my anger, though, I also felt grateful Grandma Gini had known him to be sober in the end, even if their relationship hadn't fully recovered from his years of addiction.

My phone rang. It was Dad.

"What's wrong? What's wrong?" he asked. "Is everything okay?"

"I have bad news, Dad." There was no way around it. I would have to tell him. "It's your mom. She died."

I heard his gasp of shock through the phone. And he began to cry. I felt at a total loss. I didn't know what to do. He was the parent. I was the child. I'd never heard him cry like that before. I suddenly realized that my dad was an orphan now. His adopted father, Don, had died before I was born.

For the first time, I needed to be there for him, not the other way around. I was glad I'd already done some of my own crying so I could be strong for him at that moment.

* * *

Dick called me the next day to say that there wouldn't be a funeral.

"Steve wants to do something with his family down in Mexico."

Steve had become a preacher, and he and his wife had opened an orphanage and mission in Mexico. That was his life now. He and my dad had never been super close, but Steve—like Dick, like Lyle—never could get beyond his brother's past. *Do something with his family?* I thought. *Isn't my dad Steve's family too?*

"She wanted to be cremated," Dick added.

His message was clear: *Day isn't a part of this family any longer. He has no say in our decisions.*

Yet another blow I'd have to deliver to my dad. *He wasn't even invited to his own mother's burial.* I knew that whatever inkling of a relationship between my dad and Steve still existed would be extinguished after this. It wouldn't stand a chance. Not anymore.

How could a man like my father not feel this rejection deeply? His birth mother gave him away. His wife left him. Both his adoptive parents died. His stepfathers didn't like him. And now his only sibling was ostracizing him. One by one, he had lost his whole family.

I was all he had left.

* * *

The next year I finally joined the International Soundex Reunion Registry (ISSR), which Lee from PACER had told me about. I filled out one form for my dad, which I had him sign as the adoptee, and another for myself as the birth family member, and I mailed them both in. That information would get added to their database. Everytime a new person entered, the computer would scan for similar names or dates.

As Lee had told me, I was lucky I knew my dad's birth name. Maybe something would turn up.

* * *

But when, a year later in 1998, nothing had turned up, I went back through the materials I had.

There was the 1948 letter Virginia Whitley had written to Grandma Gini. There was her return address in San Francisco. There was a direct line to Dad's birth mother! Why had I never done anything with it?

I wrote her a short letter explaining my search and asking for any information. Grandma Gini had lived in her house in Walnut Creek for decades—wasn't it possible that Virginia Whitley might still live at 1441 Ellis Street in room 610? I put her name on the envelope and underneath it wrote: *Or person living at this address.* Maybe if Virginia Whitley had moved, the person currently living in room 610 might know her whereabouts. I crossed my fingers and popped it in the mailbox.

But two weeks later, my mail carrier returned the letter, unopened. Stamped across the envelope in block letters was *No such number.*

I found out later that when Virginia Whitley had written to Grandma Gini, she was a student living in dorm room 610 at Glad Tidings Bible College. Just two years later, the college moved its campus from San Francisco to Scotts Valley. The address 1441 Ellis Street is now technically home to a church called Glad Tidings San Francisco, but they use an adjacent street as their official address.

Despite the disappointment of not finding Virginia Whitley nearby, I must have felt a renewed sense of purpose because I really dug into my research that year.

I found out that families could petition the courts (see note at end of chapter) to not only unseal original birth certificates but also open adoption files. Remember, the birth certificate I had from Grandma Gini declared that Don and Virginia Horner were the birth parents of Dayton Louis Horner. Lies! I was determined to get my hands on the original so I could find my blood grandfather's name and anything else about Virginia Whitley that might prove useful.

So I ordered copies of my dad's birth certificate from the County Recorder's Office, but I was really sneaky. Instead of asking for the original certificate for Dayton Louis Horner, I requested that of Gary Vick Whitley, born April 20, 1948, in Santa Clara County. Maybe whoever was opening the requests wouldn't realize—fifty years later—that he had been adopted and just provide the certificate!

The petition asked for reasons the petitioner wanted to open the adoption file. I wrote something along the lines of, *Purely for ancestry reasons. We will not bother the birth mother, as she would be in her seventies now and surely doesn't wish to be bothered.* I hoped my clear and noble motives would touch whichever judge read my letter. But looking back, should I have made it more personal, more impassioned? I'm not sure.

A few months later, the County Records Office responded. My request for the birth certificate of one Gary Vick Whitley came back as *No record found.*

And the Department of Social Services denied my petition to open the adoption file. But I did notice there were several other sheets of paper included. I read on:

All we can provide you with, the top letter read, *is non-identifying information obtained at the time of adoption. You can also sign and add a Consent to Contact to the official adoption file. The birth mother did not provide one herself, but this would allow her to contact you, should she wish to do so.*

Despite its restrained name, *non-identifying information* turned out to be a total treasure trove of information. Within the included envelope, I learned the age, occupation, level of education, race/ethnicity, religion, physical description, hobbies, talents, marital status, medical history, and circumstances surrounding the adoption for each of my dad's birth parents.

They also included a three-page, heavily redacted medical report from the physician attending my dad's birth. It was blurred in places and really difficult to read. I can only assume it was printed directly from microfiche storage. It read like a medical questionnaire (*How was the baby's color at birth? Normal*).

This was the most information I had ever had! I was elated and spent the next few days pouring over everything.

What I learned about the birth father absolutely fascinated me. Remember, all I knew before this was that Virginia Whitley was probably a teenager and unwed at the time of the birth. But when I read the non-identifying information, I felt like I *knew him*. He came alive for me on those pages.

The birth father was Caucasian, Scotch-Dutch, and a Protestant. Born in California, he was twenty-three at the time of the adoption. His education level and special interests and information on extended family were all unknown. He had not been married before, and in 1948 he was serving as a cook in the US Navy. His physical description gave me chills. He was five-foot-five, 140 pounds, with dark brown, naturally wavy hair, blue eyes, and a fair complexion. In other words, *my father to a T.* Not only did my father *look* like his biological father, but he'd been in the military service too! I was truly astonished.

Soon, an enticing narrative began to form in my imagination. Fed by those romance novels I'd consumed as a teenager, I pictured the young sailor, docked in San Francisco for Fleet Week. Short, but masculine and strong, his beautiful wavy hair under a white cap. When he'd laid his piercing blue eyes on lovely Virginia Whitley, he felt struck by lightning. They'd spent a few happy days (and nights) together, unable to resist each other's charms. When the week ended, he headed back to the Pacific, leaving her with promises of their future (and an unexpected son on the way).

She'd been forced to give up the child because, really, what was she to do? They weren't married, and he was still at sea. Someday, though, she'd find that child again. After they married and had a little money, she'd find him.

But when I looked back over all the information I now had, despite the romantic narrative I could enjoy, what did I really have? I still had no current address for Virginia Whitley, no record of the actual birth certificate, and no father's name.

It felt like I was hitting wall after wall.

* * *

The late nineties were eventful in my personal life. I was no longer working at the collection agency and had found my forever job, where I still work today. Joe's father got cancer and died, and then, not two years later, his mother got cancer too. I moved in with them to help Joe take care of her, but she died within a few weeks. Then, early in 1999, we got pregnant with our first daughter, and in November, we became parents—just shy of the new millennium.

I relished being a mother, but it left me little time to do anything but care for our daughter and try to stay on top of my job. Besides, the disappointments of the previous year of research had taken some of the wind out of my sails.

In 2000, though, I learned about the Social Security Death Index. You could order copies of dead people's original Social Security applications. What if Virginia Whitley had died? It pained me to think about, after all I'd done, but I pushed on. I now had the internet at home, which made my research much easier. Not only were many records now at my fingertips, but I had the luxury of logging on for a few minutes while the baby slept.

Unfortunately, Virginia Whitley didn't turn up much. I simultaneously felt relief that maybe she was still alive but also deep frustration. *Where was this woman?* At least if she was dead, I'd know *something.* I switched to searches for V. Whitley, born in California around 1920. My plan was to take signatures from the applications and compare them to the signature in the original letter to Grandma Gini.

Many of the V. Whitleys came back as Vernons or Victors. But all the other signatures looked more or less the same to me. I swear, all people born in this era have the same darned style of cursive writing.

So I gave up on the Social Security Death Index.

* * *

In 2003, Joe and I had our second child. Despite the chaos of life with two small children, I would occasionally research in my spare time (whatever that was in those days!). I wanted terribly to give more of my time to it. I would have loved to be doing genealogy and ancestry research full time. It lit a fire under me like no other work ever had.

Every time I got back into it, I would *really* get back into it. I loved how as soon as one door closed, another door would open. One clue could lead to five more. It was thrilling. And the internet in the early 2000s made everything more fun.

I found the group Search Angels (SearchAngels.org). At the time, their services were free, which was just what I needed (diapers aren't cheap!). I registered our family and searched for

Dayton Louis Horner and Gary Vick Whitley. But nothing turned up.

Today, Search Angels is a "non-profit organization here to assist you with your genealogy and DNA test results for those seeking help unraveling the past in search of their biological family roots." Back in 2003, of course, online DNA searches were still just fantasy science.

I found Adoption.com, which was (and still is) primarily a site for information about the adoption process from both sides.

One organization, though, that I absolutely loved discovering was Bastard Nation (BastardNation.org). Their work for adoptee rights is truly inspiring.

> **BASTARD NATION'S MISSION STATEMENT**
>
> Bastard Nation is dedicated to the recognition of the full human and civil rights of adult adoptees. Toward that end, we advocate the opening to adoptees, upon request at age of majority, of those government documents which pertain to the adoptee's historical, genetic, and legal identity, including the unaltered original birth certificate and adoption decree. Bastard Nation asserts that it is the right of people everywhere to have their official original birth records unaltered and free from falsification, and that the adoptive status of any person should not prohibit him or her from choosing to exercise that right. We have reclaimed the badge of bastardy placed on us by those who would attempt to shame us; we see nothing shameful in having been born out of wedlock or in being adopted. Bastard Nation does not support mandated mutual consent registries or intermediary systems in place of unconditional open records, nor any other system that is less than access on demand to the adult adoptee, without condition, and without qualification.

I also returned to the non-identifying information again and again over the years. Each time different components stood out to me.

For instance, the redacted medical report. There was no hospital listed, but a Dr. Leslie Magoon was mentioned as the presiding physician. Was it possible he or she was still around?

Online I found an article about doctors in Naglee Park that mentioned a Dr. Magoon. It was essentially a nostalgia piece on the old hospitals in the area, what types of people used to live there, and how the neighborhood had changed over the years. That was it. Locked door. I considered petitioning the area hospitals for their records, but I never got around to it.

I also re-discovered that Virginia Whitley had three sisters. The paperwork stated, "She had three sisters, ages thirty-one, twenty-three, and seventeen. They were all in good general health. Her seventeen-year-old sister was born blind. There is no information in the case about the specific cause of her blindness."

Now wait a minute, I thought. *Three whole sisters! If I can't find Virginia Whitley, could I find at least one of her sisters? They were my dad's biological aunts, after all.*

Where might they lead?

KNOWING WHAT I KNOW NOW

In the nineties I spent a lot of time writing and mailing letters and speaking on the phone. It was slow work and I would sometimes wait months for a response.

But still, I have to say, even with all the speed and incredible resources that our technology today makes possible, sometimes you just have to pick up the phone and talk to a real person. All the organizations I discovered are run by people who *really* care. They love what they do and they want to help. Many people at genealogy societies are older and are a wealth of information. Conversations make the process real, and you truly never know how much one person might be able to help you.

You should also go to your public library. There are ancestry books with family histories, and you can flip through them. Not everything is indexed for the web. Sometimes, you will just have to do the leg work because the old research practices still have merit. As surprising as it is, many, many people simply don't have internet footprints.

A few years ago, I was doing some research on my family, the Latimers, in Tennessee. I kept calling courthouses, trying to find more information. Finally, one lady on the phone said, "Wait, you're looking for a Latimer?"

"Um, yes, that's right."

"Well, you need to talk to Tommy Latimer. He knows absolutely everything about Latimers in this area."

"Does he have an email or cell phone?"

"Oh, no, sweetie. You're gonna have to call that man."

So I found his home number in an online phone directory and cold called him. I've since gone to Tennessee and met him twice. I've been included at family reunions, and he's shown me the graves of my ancestors.

Sometimes the Tommys of the world trump anything on the internet.

Lastly, your life comes first, and researching can be all-enveloping. Make sure you take time for you and your family. The research will still be there when you get to it, so be sure to give yourself grace and forgiveness if you have to take a break.

A NOTE ABOUT PETITIONING

I found it very confusing to figure out the right way to petition. There seemed to be contradictory information about whether you should petition—in the county where the adoption took place or where you live. Alma and Pacer helped me, though, explaining, "Petition the superior court of the county where you live. Your petition should be filed under the Health and Safety Code Section 102705 in the County Clerk's Office of the Superior Court to get access to the original birth certificate. File a petition under Family Code Section 9200 in the Superior Court of the county where the adoption was finalized to gain access to documents contained in the adoption file that is maintained by the Superior Court. It is the sole discretion of the Court to grant or deny this request."

So my letters read something like the following. They officially came from my dad, even though I wrote them:

> Superior Court of Contra Costa,
>
> I would like to petition the court to unseal and mail to me my "original birth certificate." I was adopted in 1948. My birth mother is about seventy years old now and, honestly, probably no longer living. I do not wish to interrupt her life, but I would just like a copy of my "original birth certificate." I believe that I can petition the court under Health and Safety Code Section 102705 and that you would graciously comply by unsealing my "original birth certificate" to me. I have enclosed the necessary forms. Please consider my request. I am a fifty year old man and would like to have my *real* information to pass down to my children and grandchildren. I feel there is a missing link in my life and heritage that I am desperately trying to find. Please consent to the request. It would make this grown man very happy.
>
> Sincerely,
>
> Dayton L. Horner

Chapter 4

SISTERS AND LIES

—

IN 1978 THE US CONGRESS PASSED A NEW LAW CONcerning our national census: information collected each decade could only be released publicly after seventy-two years had passed from the date of collection.

Why seventy-two years, you might ask? There are various theories about this today, but this span had already become customary in the 1940s and 1950s (for the publications of the 1870 and 1880 census) when the average life expectancy was closer to sixty-eight years. What better way to convince census respondents that they could afford to be *honest* in the census? By the time it would be made public, they would likely be dead. As would their nosy neighbors—who might be *very* interested to learn their actual income, that they'd been married before, or that maybe they hadn't actually served in the war, as they'd been claiming for years at cocktail parties.

But there are also weightier reasons for keeping such information private. Consider, for example, the consequences in 2001 of being able to know the home addresses of everyone living in the US who was of Afghani descent...

But a census is useless if its collected data isn't accurate. So the "72-Year Rule," as it became known, has remained an important factor in encouraging respondents to be honest.

It wasn't until 2002, therefore, that the 1930 census was made public. I, of course, was focused on raising small children, and my research was sporadic at best. So it would be another year before I got around to examining that census.

But what I discovered within it would prove to be a mess of lies and even more confusing threads for me to follow.

* * *

I knew from the non-identifying information from my court-petitioned adoption records that Virginia Whitley was living in California and had three unnamed sisters who were all in good health, although one was born blind. That—and Grandma Gini's note that Virginia Whitley was in a home for unwed mothers at the time of the adoption—were all I had to go on.

If Virginia was a teenager, as I assumed, then there was only the slimmest chance that the 1930 census would even list her as having been born, since she gave birth to my dad in 1948. But maybe, I reasoned, I could at least learn more about her parents and sisters—if they were older.

Through Ancestry.com I searched the 1930 census for a family of Whitleys living in California. Since this census had been published for a few years, it was mostly fully indexed and fairly easy to search. Indexing will probably get faster over time, of course, as AI further develops. But back in 2002, when the 1930 census was first released, it wasn't immediately searchable. This makes sense when you consider why. When the census was first taken, census takers were going from house to house, certainly not alphabetically by family. You can even see in the data where they would finish one day and start up collecting again the next. So when you first search a census, unless you know the address of the person you're looking for, you're going to end up with pages and pages of unorganized information. Imagine trying to find someone in an unalphabetized phonebook![1]

But there she was: Virginia Whitley, two years old, living with her mother (Bessie Hammond Whitley), father (Francis "Frank" Marion Whitley) and two older sisters: Marjorie, age fourteen, and Imogene, age six. I assumed her third sister hadn't been born yet. They lived in Visalia, California.

So Virginia was two in 1930! That meant she'd actually been *twenty* when she gave my dad up for adoption. I thought she'd been a pregnant teenager. Although this new information explained why she was living at a college at the time, her being *twenty* struck me as particularly interesting. Getting married at twenty would have been commonplace in 1948. In fact, according to the US Census Bureau, the average marrying age for women in 1950 was 20.3 years. Why hadn't she just married the father and kept the baby? Even if he *was* in the Navy, marriage would have been quite possible. The war was over, after all.

Had he abandoned her? Had their families not supported the union? From the non-identifying information, I knew he hadn't died and that neither of them were already married. Or maybe, her decision to give the baby up had nothing to do with the father. Maybe she just didn't want to be a mother at all? Maybe she had big career dreams and the baby would interfere with her education? That seemed like a more modern spin, but who knew.

---

[1] I found my dad at age two in the 1950 census living with his adopted parents in Walnut Creek. I couldn't search for Virginia Whitley because I had no idea what town or city she lived in so no idea where to start. I'm waiting for that 1950 census to be fully indexed before I start combing it for the Whitley sisters!

I checked back with the non-identifying information. The father's whereabouts were listed as "unknown." I had assumed this meant he was at sea and Virigina Whitley didn't know where he *literally* was. But maybe she truly had no idea? There was also no information listed about the father's extended family, which I hadn't given this much thought to when I first read it, but now, I wondered. How well did they know each other?

The possibilities were puzzling. *What didn't I know?*

* * *

With my access to the 1930 census, I was so hopeful I might be able to use the information about the sisters to dig deeper. But for years I just kept hitting wall after wall. I couldn't seem to find anything else on them.

Five years later, in 2008, I made a few last-ditch efforts.

I called up the *Visalia Times* and placed a classified ad. I've always wondered what the woman on the other end of the phone, taking my copy, must have thought. I suppose it probably wasn't the *strangest* classified they'd ever received, but still. It makes me chuckle looking back at what I wrote: But I was *desperate* to find these sisters!

> **SEARCHING** for Virginia, Imogene & Marjorie Whitley of Visalia. *Family urgency!* If you know them, please call **925-**▓▓▓▓▓▓▓▓

My classified ad in the *Visalia Times*

No one ever called me. The number I gave was our home landline. Had someone tried when we were out of the house and hung up? I'll never know.

Through Ancestry.com, I found a number of Whitleys, who listed their contact information. I reached out to them, just asking if they could fill in the blanks to what I did know. I didn't mention adoption, only that I hoped to collaborate with other genealogists. No one seemed connected to Virginia or her sisters.

> Initially a family tree maker, *Ancestry.com* also provides official records that you can tap into for free. Upgrades give you access to even more records, like international ones. The site allows you to connect to other people's family trees. You can make your tree public or private and searchable or unsearchable. Mine are public because I want to collaborate. Living people in public trees are not shown with their names. Only the dead show up as named.

Finally, I mailed letters to any Virginia Whitley I could find on the internet who was born in or around 1928 to 1930. I must have sent at least a dozen letters all over the United States, but responses were far and few between. Nothing was helpful.

Now I was at a total loss. *Where was Virginia Whitley?* What had happened to her after she gave my dad up? And why on earth couldn't I find her?

I was just a hobbyist. I didn't have the fancy, paid subscriptions. I had learned how to do skip tracing from being a debt collector at one point, but I didn't personally have that technology.

But I was closer than I realized. Once it clicked what I needed to do, pieces began to fall into place. One month in 2009 would prove the most consequential in all of my research. That was when everything would change.

But before I get into all that, I want to share my later research on Virginia Whitley's sisters. In many ways, it is this research on the sisters that has been the strangest and most enigmatic of it all.

* * *

In 2012, the US Census Bureau released the 1940 census to the public. You can just imagine how eagerly I had been waiting for this year to arrive! It was here that I made some startling discoveries.

By 1940, Bessie Whitley had passed away. I found through the California Death Index that she had passed on March 22, 1931, and the oldest sisters, Marjorie and Imogene, had moved out of the house. Frank Whitley had remarried—to a woman named Jenny who was from Sweden. The census listed Virginia as still living at home, but where was that third sister, who I knew to be blind? I had assumed from the 1930 census that she hadn't been born yet, but now I learned that her mother had died in 1931. *So where was she?*

Using the mother's maiden name, Bessie Hammond, I searched for any baby Whitley born around 1930 in Tulare county, California. And voilá! There was one Frances Marion Whitley, born in 1930. It had to be her, the third sister of Virginia. After all, Tulare Country was a sparsely populated farming community at the time. Public birth records don't record blindness or other disabilities, so I couldn't confirm it was her, but what were the chances—especially given her middle name, the same as Frank's—that it was *not* her?

But then, within that 1940 census, I found a Frances Marion Whitley living at the Institute for the Blind in Berkeley. Bessie had died six months after Frances was born, which explained why Bessie wasn't included in the 1940 census and why Frances wasn't included in the 1930 census. Then, at some point, Frank had sent her to live at the institute. But that is more or less where my research on Frances ended. At one point I thought I might have found out where she got married and worked as a legal secretary, but I couldn't be certain. And in one or two documents I found, she was listed as a boy by mistake (perhaps due to an error with the traditional spelling of her name). I have reached out to blind institutes in California, but they have yet to return my calls.

I moved on to the oldest sister, Marjorie. On Ancestry.com, I actually found a ton of information. Apparently, she was something of a famous person in Windsor, California. She appeared to be a community service icon, serving on several boards and connected with various other volunteer organizations. Her retirement party was well publicized.

But she lived in Windsor! I couldn't believe it. Marjorie was only a ninety-minute car ride from me and hadn't died until 2000. If I had acted on the info I knew about her in 1998—that in 1938 she was twenty-one and married Ernest King, as per the California Marriage Index and the local papers—perhaps I would have been able to meet her.

I did, however, discover that Marjorie had been married a few times and had several children. I started researching her children in my spare time. She had one child still alive: Ernestine, who was in her seventies and seemed to be living in the same house Marjorie had lived in. What amazing convenience! I told myself I'd get to it later, given she was still alive and I had a known address.

It wasn't until 2018 that I finally wrote Ernestine a letter and introduced myself. I told her about my father's adoption but that I hadn't been able to learn much about the circumstances around the adoption or about the biological father. Did she have any information about her mother's sister, Virginia, that she'd be willing to share?

Ernestine, who was now in her eighties, turned out to be the sweetest lady. She wrote me back, opening her heart and entire family history to me. She sent me so many family pictures, including one of Frances with a white cane. Later in our correspondence, I learned that her mother, Marjorie, was not, in fact, the biological child of Frank and Bessie Whitley, making her not a biological sister of Virginia. So the 1930 census was inaccurate! The Whitleys had listed her as a biological child living with them. But they had actually adopted her from a Bertha Frame. Bertha was known as a wild woman in their county, who had lots of babies that she gave to other people.

"I don't care if we're not blood related," Ernestine told me once. "I consider us cousins!" Same, Ernestine. Same. Marjorie, moreover, actually had Ernestine out of wedlock, and Ernestine grew up not knowing her biological father at all. She was raised by a stepfather. So with her permission, I looked into it and found the information for her. She said, "You've told me more than my own mother did!"

Also in 2018, I had my DNA processed through 23andMe. I soon found a close match with a Seth W.[2] We shared a number of connections—enough to pique my interest. Twenty years my junior, he was the great-grandson of Imogene. I reached out to him over the platform, explaining my research and asking about the Whitley sisters. We began communicating.

Seth confirmed that Imogene Whitley was indeed his great-grandmother and that her daughter, Bonnie, was his grandmother. He kindly put us in touch, and through him—because I was concerned that Bonnie might think I was a crazy person—I began corresponding with her. Eventually, she and I continued our conversations independently of Seth, and she flooded me with family photos, including one of Virginia Whitley as a child. She unfortunately died only six months after we met, so I was particularly grateful for the time and energy she shared with me.

But through Bonnie I also learned a few family stories. She told me that both Marjorie and Imogene had left home as teenagers, leaving Virginia and Frances behind. Eventually, Virginia was put into foster care, and Frances was sent to the Institute for the Blind. It sounded to me like Frank Whitey really struggled to raise his daughters without Bessie. But Virginia Whitley in foster care! This explained in part why it'd been so difficult for me to find her.

---

2   23andMe disclosed his full name.

Furthermore, Imogene Whitley had a son, Jimmy, whom she gave up for adoption. She had simply dropped the baby off at her older sister Marjorie's house for a while (Ernestine remembers this time). I can imagine that Marjorie, who was so involved in the community and had so many children herself, would have been more than capable of handling the situation. But then Imogene returned for baby Jimmy, only to give him to a local preacher and his wife. Imogene later tried to get Jimmy back from them, but they refused. Imogene eventually got on with her life, married, had Bonnie, and moved to Montana.

Through 23andMe I've reached out to Jimmy and his wife but received no response. Ernestine sent him letters, but he never responded. Bonnie told me that she and Jimmy had met a few times but have since lost touch.

It's amazing to me now, looking back on those short six months that Bonnie and I corresponded. We were utterly unguarded. Talking to her felt so natural, like talking to an aunt. It never felt like she was a stranger, but like we'd known each other for years.

But once I had so much information, I very clearly remember thinking at the time, *Man, what is up with these Whitley sisters?*

Marjorie herself was adopted. She then had Ernestine out of wedlock and kept her. Imogene gave up her son, Jimmy (conceived out of wedlock with an unknown man). And Virginia gave up her son Gary/Dayton (conceived out of wedlock with an unknown man). Even by today's more relaxed expectations around children, marriage, and adoption, that would be extraordinary—three out of four sisters in one family. Amazing. And who knew—maybe enigmatic Frances had joined this club too!

What struck me as most interesting, though, was one shocking truth.

No one seemed to know that Virginia had even been pregnant with my dad, much less given him up for adoption. No one living who I'd been in touch with was able to provide any information at all. Typical! I finally uncover some truths, but they only lead to a dozen more questions.

But that was all about to change. And fast.

Virginia and Frances

Marjorie in 1986

Imogene and Bonnie, 1943

KNOWING WHAT I KNOW NOW

For years, I believed everything I read. Don't.

It's important to maintain a healthy level of skepticism and remember that despite the protection of the 72-Year Rule, people still lie on census surveys (and hospital records, as I later discovered). Try to keep an open mind that you might find out new information that will disprove your original theory.

Marjorie married two or three times, had a huge family, was in the newspapers frequently, and lived near me. I should have been able to find her easily before she died. But I procrastinated because I was living the rest of my life and didn't have the time. If you *do* have the time, jump on any leads you have. Make the drive! Knock on doors!

You never know who you're going to connect with and enrich your life. There was apparently a lot of sister drama between the Whitley sisters, so both Ernestine and Bonnie were overjoyed to find me. Ernestine now considers me family.

Write down your theories, no matter how ridiculous they may seem. Follow up on them till you can't follow up anymore. Your first instinct might be true, or it might be romanticizing. As I would discover, I had completely romanticized the relationship between my dad's biological parents.

Organization is key. Keep your notes organized by person: everything you know, everything you still need to know, and tasks to follow up.

As with anything involving problem-solving, taking breaks in your research can be critical. You never know what new perspective or fresh idea you've never considered may come about because you were able to clear your mind.

Even in the 2000s, I was searching for Virginia Whitley—her maiden name. I never stopped to consider whether she had married. And all that *Whitley* searching was getting me nowhere.

Chapter 5

THE TRUTH

—

I WAS PROUD OF ALL THE RESEARCH I'D DONE OVER the past seventeen years.

From cold calling distant relatives to petitioning the courts to placing classified ads, my work had run the gamut. And despite the fact that I still hadn't found Virginia Whitley—my own flesh-and-blood grandmother—I was determined to keep at it.

But it felt like I'd been beating my head against locked door after locked door. There was one key I knew might unlock the mystery. But I didn't want to use it. Not yet. Maybe never. It felt like cheating. I'd come this far on my own, and I desperately wanted to complete the research entirely on my own. Nothing would have made me happier or given me a greater sense of accomplishment. If I'm being honest, it felt like it was my *right* to solve the mystery on my own.

Besides, I had lingering doubts that it would be worth the money. I'd tapped all the resources, hadn't I? What if I paid all this money and nothing popped up?

But by the end of 2008, those locked doors got to me. My frustration had peaked. So I caved.

I hired a private investigator to find Virginia Whitley.

* * *

This option had actually been on my mind for a while. About a decade before, I'd needed to look into someone in my life, so I hired a private investigator through the company Worldwide Tracers. They were specialists in missing persons records, Homeland Security background checks, employment background checks, and arrest records. In other words, everything a regular citizen wouldn't have access to. They had helped me with that person, and I was impressed with their professionalism and thoroughness.

So I looked them up and called. They were based in Texas.

They soon connected me with a woman named Monda, who was the lead investigator of adoptions. We emailed back and forth for a while as I filled her in, sharing everything I knew so far. My biggest fear, I think, was that she'd just come back to me with redundant information.

Then, eventually, we spoke on the phone.

"Okay, Jennifer, you asked about opening the adoption records?"

"Yes! That would be really great." I wasn't entirely sure of the extent of Monda's investigative and legal powers, but who knew? I was hopeful.

"Unfortunately, even though we're in Texas, we still have to abide by California adoption laws."

Figured. How disappointing. But my head was used to banging against a closed door, so I barreled right ahead. "Well," I said, "I have two priorities then."

"Go ahead."

"First, I want to find Virginia Whitley. I don't even know if she's dead or alive. And second, I'd like as much information about her sisters as you can find."

"Will do."

I then started listing everything I knew again. And emphasizing my priorities. It felt monumentally important that she listen to me. I was so worried she'd come back to me with something like, "Guess what! Virginia Whitley once lived at 1441 Ellis Street in San Francisco!" or "And one sister was blind!"

Please, no, I thought.

"Wow," Monda replied in her Texas drawl when I wrapped up my litany of facts. "You have so much information. This is going to be easy!"

Rude, I thought. Her chipper, confident tone irritated me. If it was so easy, why hadn't I found them yet? But of course, I didn't have access to the same databases she did.

After that, I called or emailed Monda every week to check on my inquiry's status. It felt like an eternity. If it was so easy, why was it taking so long?

For a while, she stopped responding. I couldn't really blame her for that—I'm sure I was annoying. But I was just so dang eager!

But then, three months later, in early February of 2009, she got back to me. The official report would be sent to me later, but we scheduled a phone call so she could tell me their findings.

When I answered Monda's call at work, my heart was already thumping. But I had no idea what a roller coaster of a ride she was about to take me on.

"We found quite a lot," she began.

A lot! Oh my god. I braced myself.

"Virginia Whitley married Wilford Frazier, and they lived in Washington state. That's why you were having trouble finding her—she changed her name and moved out of state."

She got married. All this time I'd been searching for a Whitley. Why, why, why had I been so hyper-focused on Whitley? It never occurred to me that she might have married. All this time I'd had a very specific vision of Virginia Whitley: unmarried, living alone, pining away for the baby she gave away all those years ago. I'd had such tunnel vision. But they had found her! My hopes began to rise.

"But Jennifer? Virginia Frazier died in 1991."

My heart just about plummeted. 1991. That was the year that my interest renewed and my search truly began. I never even had a chance. I never would have had the opportunity to meet her. Or reconnect her with her son. I just sat silently on the phone, heartbroken. It was never meant to be. All that work, all those years. Grandma Gini told me about her in 1987. Why didn't I start looking sooner? I would have had four years! I was so angry and disappointed in myself.

Monda must have realized what was going on with my silence. Or at least she knew enough from her experience to wait patiently while the news sank in.

"There's something else, though," she said, after a few moments. "Virginia had a son in 1953. His name is Max Frazier, and he lives in Texas."

That hit me like a sledgehammer. *She had another son? A son she…kept. How dare she?* For a few breaths, I took in shock and anger and hurt. How dare she give my dad up for adoption and then, just a few years later, move on with her life! What an awful woman. How could she do that?

But soon I got control of my senses. My anger began to subside. The fault wasn't with Virginia Whitley, of course. It was with me. What was I thinking? That she would just be alone the rest of her life—waiting for her son to find her? Sitting elegantly like Pearl before a lace-curtained window, hoping day in and day out that he might stroll up the walk and embrace her?

Virginia Whitley was twenty. She had a whole life ahead of her. I couldn't believe how much I had allowed my romantic vision of her to blind me.

"Okay," was all I could manage to say aloud.

"I have a PO box for his address in Azle, Texas, that I can give you. Looks like he owns a business of some kind."

She gave me the address, waited, and finally added, "Did you get all that?"

"Um, yeah. I think so." I stared at the address in front of me.

"Do you have any questions?"

I felt like I was grasping for a response. I was expecting to find a mother and three aunts. *But another son?* I wasn't expecting any of this.

"Can you, um, tell me if he's a good guy?" I stammered out. "Like, does he have a criminal record or something? Do you know if he's a deadbeat or an asshole?"

Monda laughed. "He lives in Azle, Texas. There aren't any deadbeats or assholes in Azle, honey."

* * *

When Joe walked in the door from work that evening, I practically assaulted him with everything I'd learned.

"You're never going to believe what I found out today!"

He listened, amazed, as I told him all about Virginia Frazier and her son Max. After all, he'd been on this journey with me for all of these years.

But then I told him what I'd been mulling over on the drive home. *Should I reach out to Max?* The question played over and over in my head. Of course I'd planned to reach out to Virginia Whitley when I found her. But should I do the same with Max?

Joe just looked at me and said, "Be careful, Jennifer."

He was right. Max could be a creep or a murderer—Azle resident or no. We had two daughters and a happy home. Would I be subjecting myself to someone who could harm us? What did I really know about this guy? Or what if he thought *I* was the creepy gold digger?

Virginia was dead now. I would never find her. And when I finally received the official report from Worldwide Tracers, they had nothing of real substance to add about the sisters. All of that I would discover on my own, as I mentioned in the previous chapter.

But Virginia's son, Max, was an actual, living blood brother to my dad. What if—after all this—I found him a new brother, and then he rejected us? I think I feared this above all else. It was a narrative I just couldn't process. How would I feel if someone approached me out of the blue claiming to be the daughter of my long-lost sister?

My dad had often told me that he had a local girlfriend when he was over in Vietnam. "Maybe," he would say, only somewhat joking, "you've got a sibling out there!" But those kinds of suggestions have a certain staying power in the imagination. Even today, I half expect a sibling to show up on my doorstep.

But if they ever did show up, at least Dad had told me it was a possibility. Did Max know about his older brother, Day? And, if he did, did he even care? Did he want a brother? I had just assumed from Monda's report that he was an only child. What if Virginia had had more? Or what if he had a terrible relationship with his mother and wanted nothing else to do with her or anything that was hers? Or what if it was the opposite? What if he worshipped the ground she'd walked on but she had lied to him about the adoption and learning about Day would shatter his image of her?

Virginia Whitley Frazier knew she had a child and gave him up. She knew he was out there in the world and that the possibility—however slim—remained that they might cross paths one day. However she felt about that possibility, she at least knew it existed.

But what about Max? Who was he as a person? What did he know? I fretted over all these questions for some time.

But there was one consideration in all of this that kept circling back to me: my dad and Steve had never been close.

And at this point, their relationship was nonexistent. My dad had been clean and sober since 1995. Fourteen whole years. He'd completely turned his life around. From PTSD clinics to therapy to AA, he'd done the hard work. Over and over. He was also deeply, passionately involved in the recovery community. He mentored and sponsored. Everyone knew and looked up to him. He was a good citizen. He'd even won the prestigious Normadene Carpenter Award, which was given annually by Arts and Culture El Dorado to recognize extraordinary commitment to culture and creativity.

Dad's award

But, according to my dad, none of this was ever good enough for Steve, who thought he was—and always would be—a deadbeat. Steve was pretty severe when it came to Christianity too: walk in the land of God and join his ministry, or you were out. But Dad wasn't into that. He believed in a higher power (you had to in AA, after all), but he didn't necessarily believe it was God. They were both believers, but Steve and Dad always struck me as representatives of two very different sides of faith: judgment and mercy. If someone didn't go to church, Steve would say, "See, that's your problem right there." Whereas Dad would say, "Okay, you do you, man."

I don't really know what their relationship was like before Grandma Gini died. We'd get together at her house for Christmas with Steve, his wife Cathy, and my two cousins. I had a great time with all of them. I really loved my cousins. I never saw any fights between Steve and Dad. But I always sensed Dad was uncomfortable. He was the divorced guy with a weekend kid, and at that time he was still dealing with PTSD and addiction. But after he got straight, he realized he didn't want a relationship with anyone who judged him so much. And Steve, for his own reasons, felt the same way.

They were only three years apart in age, but they'd just never really had a good connection. For weeks I thought about this. And I thought about Max.

And then I knew what I had to do.

KNOWING WHAT I KNOW NOW

We all want our happy ending. We don't want to be let down. We want our fantasy stories to delight us with their coming true. "See?" we want these romanticized visions to say. "You were right all along! This is just how it was. You *are indeed* the daughter of a prince, just as you suspected."

I felt this way too. And I was the granddaughter, not even the actual adoptee!

My best advice, therefore, is to try to hold—simultaneously—both the fairy tale ending and also the more realistic outcomes. Don't give up hope for the fairy tale ending. If you did, what would be the point of research in the first place? But also know that sometimes that fantasy vision can actually impede your research and that some disappointment is probably inevitable.

My own fantasy of Virginia—never moving on with her life, simply pining away—impeded my search. I couldn't ever think outside that very small box I had placed her in.

But of course, not everything is within your control. Sometimes unexpected turns impede your search too. For instance, once I knew the names Wilford and Virginia Frazier, I was able to find their obituaries. It was in Virginia's obituary that I learned a fascinating puzzle piece: she had been placed with a foster family, the Corsaws, as a teenager. As it turned out, the Corsaws would play a significant, rather darker role in all this story—but I discovered that much later.

I had so much against me: Virginia Whitley had lived with a foster family, had married and moved out of state, and had died! I never anticipated any of this. And *all* of it would have changed how I'd searched for her, if I'd only known.

Discovering that she had died just a few years after my search began was devastating, and I was very hard on myself for a while. But looking back, what could I have done? The internet was still a decade away, and I was just a poor young adult, trying to discover my own way in the world. I certainly couldn't have afforded a private investigator back in those days.

So if the timing feels tragic, try not to be too hard on yourself. You tried when most people never do.

And, as I was about to discover, you just never know what incredible and unexpected gifts might await you around the next corner.

Chapter 6

ARE YOU SITTING DOWN?

AS I DISCOVERED OVER THE YEARS, THERE ARE MANY painful stigmas surrounding adoption.

A common stigma, of course, concerns the hierarchy of biology, as if *biology and realness are one and the same.* The birth mother is the *real* mother, and the adoptive mother is less than real, or whatever a step below real is.

Another common stigma, which seems to ironically contradict the first, is about secrecy, as if *any secrecy surrounding an adoption ought to remain secret.* Birth parents gave up their child for a "good reason." The mother was sixteen at the time and her family didn't want it "to get out." Skeletons need to stay in closets. Sleeping dogs need to lie. So when adoptees try to find their birth parents, there's often an undeserved pressure on them *to stop*: stop bothering the parents, stop interrupting their life, stop trying to open up old wounds.

But as I frequently read on online chat boards, many adoptees feel strongly about this. *We're not secrets*, they would say. *We were innocent in all of this. We did nothing wrong.* And the rallying cry of adoptee advocates everywhere: *We deserve to know. It is our right.*

* * *

I had decided to contact Max.

Nevertheless, a host of contradicting thoughts swirled around my head. Would I be disrupting his life? Would I open wounds? What if he was a total jerk? Did I deserve—as his biological niece—to know the truth?

And, of course, I mostly worried that Max would ignore or reject us. Although my father had never shown any interest in my search, the last thing I wanted was for him to experience yet another rejection. I'd occasionally update him on my findings ("I found some census records" and the like), but he never showed any real curiosity. What if I told him about Max's existence—a real, live brother—and then it was all for nothing?

I determined that I would sniff out Max first and then decide what to tell Dad.

I typed up a letter to him and copied a number of photos of my dad onto 8.5 x 11 sheets. I included baby, elementary, and high school photos and one from his wedding at twenty-four. I also included a current photo of him and one of me.

I knew I needed to include enough information and detail in the letter to convince Max of both my sincerity and also the truth of our connection. But it also felt like I was walking a bit of a tightrope: I didn't want to scare him away with too much information or too much emotional baggage. It was important to me that he understood I wasn't seeking anything other than information, not even necessarily a relationship. I certainly didn't want him to think I was a crazy person trying to extort money from him.

February 5, 2009

Dear Mr. Frazier,

I am writing to you in the belief that you are my birth-Uncle. My dad was given up for adoption by your mother, Virginia Whitley, in 1948-49 in San Jose, CA. Virginia had named the baby Gary Vick Whitley at birth. He was adopted by the Horner's in 1949 and his name was changed upon adoption. I know that back in that time, birth mothers were told to keep these types of things a secret so your mother may have never told your father, or you, about her other child. However, your Aunt's Imogene and Marjorie did know about the baby and the adoption, as did Virginia's father, Frank.

It's very difficult to know how to start this letter, as I certainly don't want to cause problems in your life. I can appreciate that this letter while half expected may come as a great shock to you, and you may be wondering how it will all turn out. I am also aware that your family and friends may not know about this and that may pose great difficulties for you. I'd like to reassure you that I have thought long and hard about writing this letter, and I would never disturb your privacy by turning up unannounced.

Nevertheless, I have many questions, about my background and where I come from, that my dad's adoptive parents are not able to answer. I was hoping that we could exchange letters and perhaps have a phone call or meeting in the future, but only if you are willing. I will certainly respect any decision you make about this, and understand that you may need some time to think it over.

Perhaps I could tell you a bit about why I've been searching and then a bit about myself. I started searching for Virginia Whitley around 1999 on behalf of my father. His adoptive parents had passed away so there was no threat or hurting their feelings. I petitioned the courts to have the adoption file opened but was denied. The courts did however send me a lot of information; that Virginia had 3 sisters, one of which was blind. Her mother died at an early age and her father remarried. Attached is a copy of the information the court gave me from the adoption case file. I have a letter from Virginia that I'm willing to share with you later if you'd like. Then you can see her handwriting as well. I'm also sending a few photos of my dad for you to see what your half-brother looks like (maybe you guys look alike?) and some photos of me and my kids. I've always wondered if I looked like my grandmother or not…?

Please ring me or write whenever you feel ready to do this. Even if you do not wish to have contact, it would be helpful for me to hear that too. I am content to wait but really need to know your wishes.

Sincerely,

Jennifer Wallig

My first letter to Max

Dad, twenty-four years old, on his wedding day

I sent the packet. And then I waited.

Two weeks. Three weeks. Four weeks went by, and still I heard nothing. The address Monda had given me was not a personal address but a PO Box for his business. What if she'd given me the wrong address? Or I'd copied it down incorrectly? I was in such shock on that phone call. Or what if his business had changed? What if the mail carrier refused to deliver it and then it got lost?

I'd given Max my home address, email, and home phone number. If he ever did reach out, how would he? I checked my mailbox religiously every afternoon. When new emails dinged in, I found myself disappointed when they weren't from Max. I couldn't wait by the phone, but I sure wanted to. The waiting was as hard as not knowing what to expect. What if he sent a letter that said, *Don't ever write to me again. I don't want to know you. Cease and desist*?

I feared the worst. And as another week passed, I began to lose hope.

In mid-March, I was at work in my office, which I shared with a coworker, Jaime. She was more than a coworker, really. We had become close friends, and I was even a bridesmaid in her wedding. Plus, since we spent nine hours a day together, I'd shared my research journey with her. She was one of my biggest cheerleaders.

An email dinged in with a heightened data security alert. I didn't immediately recognize the name. My company receives a lot of daily emails. On a heavy day, I'm sometimes looking at 300 emails, but I generally recognize the senders.

I leaned in to get a better look at the sender's name, which was only partially shown: Frazier.

I gasped out loud. Was that *him*?

"What's wrong?" Jaime asked. "You okay?"

Ding! Another email from Frazier came in. This one had an attachment.

"I—I think it's him. I think Max emailed me." I'd of course told her about the letter I sent.

"Oh my gosh! That's great. What does he say?"

I took a deep breath. "I'm about to find out."

I wanted to open the email with an attachment, but I knew I should start with the first one. So I did.

Hi Jennifer,

This is Max. I got your letter in the mail. I was quite surprised. I had no idea. I'm so surprised. But I can see a definite resemblance here. So let's talk.

I read the email again. *Okay,* I thought, *he wants to connect! He's definitely expressing shock, but he wants to connect.*

Ding! Another attachment came in.

I opened the first one. It was a—recent, I assumed—photo of Max holding up a fish he'd caught. The resemblance to my dad was uncanny. He even held the fish up the exact same way my dad always did. None of the pictures I'd sent Max showed my dad fishing. Maybe all fishermen held up their fish that same way? I didn't know. But I stared at that picture for a while. My heart was beating so fast.

One by one, more emails from Max dinged in. The attachment limit on email was so small at that time that he had to send me his photos one at a time. And then I couldn't open more than one photo at a time without my computer freezing. So I'd wait for the next photo, stare at it hungrily, and then close it down while I waited for the next to come in. It was agonizing. I wanted them all at once!

I didn't reply right away. I wanted him to finish sending all of the attachments.

I took some deep breaths to calm my nerves. I was flabbergasted. Was this really happening? Could this actually work out? I never thought this would happen. Or did I? I didn't know.

After about an hour, Max's emails stopped dinging in. It was clear he'd sent me what he planned to send. I looked through the ten photos, read his email one more time, and hit *reply*.

I wanted to say, *OMG, you guys are totally brothers!*

But I held myself back. I needed to play it cool, not wear my heart on my sleeve. At least, not yet.

> Hi Max,
>
> Oh my goodness. I'm so happy you got the letter and that you sent photos. I can't believe how much alike you all look. I saw you sent a fishing photo. Do you fish a lot?

Max replied quickly. I pictured him sitting at his computer, too, eagerly waiting for me to respond.

> Yeah, I fish a lot. I hunt, too, but not as often.

And just like that, Max and I began to correspond. Over the next few weeks, we emailed frequently. I liked what I was learning about him.

In one exchange, I asked him what he had thought when he first received my letter. He responded with a long email, describing what had happened that day.

Max had gone to the post office to collect his business mail. Seeing an unusual envelope from a Wallig in California, he immediately opened it there in the post office and started reading the letter on top.

What the heck is this? he thought and scanned to the bottom to see who it was from. He didn't recognize the name. Leaning against a wall inside the post office, he flipped through the pages of photos.

Then his eyes fell on one of eleven-year-old Dayton.

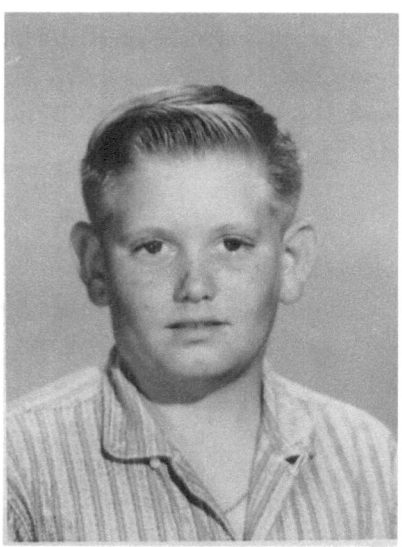

Dad, eleven years old

What on earth? Max wondered. *But that's...me.*

He went back to the top letter and read it fully this time. When he got to the end, he felt his knees buckle. He slid down the wall behind him and plopped onto the cold floor, stupefied.

Once more, he went through everything, more carefully this time. He stared at the picture of a twenty-four year-old, tuxedoed Dayton at his wedding. *I think this is real*, Max thought. The man's round, rugged face showed skin that was tanned and covered in freckles. His unruly hair shone thick and golden in the California sunshine. His large ears, rounded nose, the distinct cleft in his square chin.

There was no denying it. This man Dayton was just so... *familiar.*

Max, twelve years old

Max sat for a long time on that post office floor, speechless. When he was finally able to compose himself, he gathered up all his mail and went home.

His wife, Valerie, could tell something was up when he walked in the door. "You okay?"

"Yeah...but I got some interesting mail today." He handed her the letter.

Valerie read it. He watched the disbelief flood her face.

"Oh, Max, you can't believe this. You don't think this is real, do you? You're being scammed, surely. I mean, your mom never had any more kids. We would have known. Right?"

"Uh-huh," Max said. And then handed her the photos.

Valierie examined the sheets. Her eyes lingered for a long time on eleven-year-old Dayton and the wedding-day photo. She sat down slowly at the kitchen table.

"Max," she let out a long breath, "I think you...you have a brother."

* * *

After a few weeks of emailing back and forth, Max asked me, "Have you told your dad yet? Please feel free to give him my email and phone."

I had been so wrapped up in my correspondence with him that I'd forgotten to consider whether my dad would actually *want* to contact Max.

I trusted Max now enough that I felt safe introducing them. I sensed he was neither an asshole nor a deadbeat, and I knew he wouldn't reject my dad outright. It also seemed clear that he trusted me. Max and Valerie were devout Christians, very involved in their church ministry, and I intuited that a part of them was just going on faith that I was okay and meant no harm.

I could tell from Max's emails that he wasn't the most internet-savvy person. I doubted he or Valerie had known how to search for me or my family online.

I told Max I needed a few days, and then I would let my dad know.

* * *

I had to leave for San Francisco for a work conference. I wasn't looking forward to it, but I had to go.

Throughout a morning of mind-numbingly dull seminars, I obsessed over the phone call I knew I needed to make. *Should I sneak out the back and make it now? No, I'll wait till the lunch break. But lunch will be the only worthwhile thirty minutes in the whole day! Ugh.*

When the presenter finally droned to a close, a woman stood up and reminded us that we would take thirty minutes for lunch and meet back in this room at twelve thirty.

I filed out with the crowd into the hotel lobby, which now smelled of cheap sandwiches and pasta salad. I was starving, and I had to pee. I looked toward the women's room and saw a long line was already forming. *Double ugh.*

This was it. I needed to call Dad. I couldn't put it off any longer.

I found a small alcove off the lobby and pulled out my heavy Nokia phone. I'd put six fresh AA batteries in it that morning.

Ring.

"Hello, my beautiful daughter!"

"Hello, Faddah!"

And he sang out, "Hello, Muddah. Hello, Fadduh. Here I am at Camp Granada!"

I laughed. Typical Dad. Typical us.

"What's up, daughter? What are you up to?"

I told him about the conference.

"You're so smart. Going to conferences in San Francisco. I bet you'll be running that thing by the end of the day!"

"Hey, Dad, I have to tell you something."

"Huh? Are you pregnant again?" Typical Dad. Always the jokester.

"No, Dad. I need you to sit down." I suddenly felt really nervous. Dang it. I should have peed. "Are you sitting down?"

"Um, all right. Sure thing. Okay, I'm sitting down. What's going on?"

"Remember when I told you how I was looking for your birth mom?"

"Yeah."

"Well, I found her, but she's dead."

"Oh, okay. Well, that's too bad." Did he sound a little sad? Or just polite? I couldn't tell. I reminded myself how clear he'd made it that Grandma Gini was his mother.

"But...there's something else, Dad. You have a half brother."

"Okay."

I waited for more, but he didn't say anything else. I felt disappointed. I wanted his enthusiasm. I wanted him to express what *I'd been feeling* over the past few weeks. The excitement and wonder of discovering Max. But I realized that wasn't fair to him. This hadn't been his search. And besides, he knew nothing about him.

"So I've been talking to him."

"You have?" He sounded only mildly surprised.

"Yeah. His name is Max, and he was born in 1953." Everything I'd learned started tumbling out of me all at once. "He's actually really cool. He lives in Texas. He fishes. He plays music, and he's just into a lot of the same stuff you are. He's an only child. And we've shared photos. And Dad? He looks *exactly* like you."

"Huh! Really?" I could hear Dad perk up. "He looks like me?"

"Yeah, he really does."

I thought about that. Grandma Gini, with her delicate nose, small, smooth chin, and raven-dark hair, looked nothing like Dad. His father, Don, had no freckles and straight, easily combable blond hair. Dad looked nothing like either of his parents—neither individually nor a combination of them. He didn't look like his brother Steve or any aunts, uncles, or cousins. He just looked *different*. What would that be like? To grow up and never see your features reflected in the family around you? I mean, I looked like my dad. Everyone always told me so. But what would it be like for him to grow up and never hear that from someone?

"Joe and I agree he's a good guy." My dad loved Joe. I knew he'd trust his assessment of another guy. "Max said he'd like to talk to you sometime. Over the phone or email. Would you like that?"

"Okay."

I waited. Just *okay*? *Again*? There was no negative or positive spin to his tone. Just neutral. I was so frustrated. Men sometimes. I swear!

I checked my watch. The lunch break was nearly over. I felt my stomach rumbling, and I still had to pee. I wondered then why I'd chosen that window of time to call him. Was it some sort of self-preservation? If things went south or he didn't respond how I hoped, at least I'd have a time limit?

"I gotta get back to the conference, but I'll send you his info."

"All right, schnookums. Talk to you later. Love you."

"Love you, too, Dad."

The second half of the conference turned out to be worse than the first. Not only were the presenters somehow even more boring, but I had to sit there, hungry, the whole time. I just replayed our conversation over and over in my head. I felt immense relief that I'd finally unburdened myself of carrying the secret about Max. But still, I fretted over Dad.

Would he actually call Max? If he didn't, how would I explain it to Max? I decided that he probably would. I banked a lot on how much he'd perked up over their physical similarities.

I had this gut feeling that Dad would really like Max too. I decided to introduce them to each other over email. That way, either of them could reach out first. Plus, I'd get to witness how they first interacted.

Otherwise, I knew the curiosity would just about kill me.

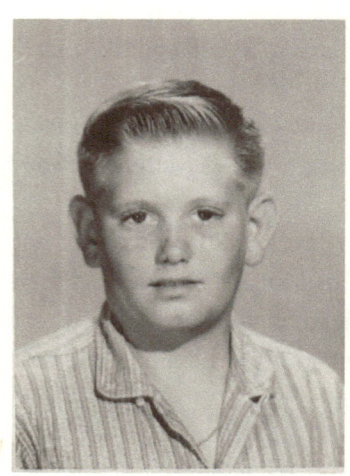

Dad, eleven years old

Max, twelve years old

Dad the cowboy

Max the cowboy

Dad the fisherman

Max the fisherman

KNOWING WHAT I KNOW NOW

For once, I wouldn't have changed a thing.

I was honest and forthcoming in my initial letter to Max. I included lots of information and proof. Where I got especially lucky, though, was that he had the right character to receive it.

Do be cautious and thoughtful, though, about the information you send. Don't send anything that isn't already easily available online. Pretend that you're meeting this person face to face and they're still a stranger (which, of course, *they are*). What would you be willing to share?

Also, be sure to think a little further down the road. What's your plan for if and when they respond? What if they reject you? Or simply don't care? What if they strike you as unstable? What if they seem a little *too excited*? What are your personal red flags, and how will you deal with them?

Have your guard up, but don't build the wall too high. There are no easy answers here for how to interact with newly discovered family. All you can do is be prepared for the various possibilities.

Chapter 7

A TRIP TO TEXAS

THERE IS A PHOTO OF MY DAD, SITTING CROSS-LEGGED in a bunker in Vietnam, guitar across his lap. He's leaning over the instrument, strumming it, totally focused. He's so young. His olive-green Marine fatigues almost look too big on him.

I love this photo because it captures his concentration in this moment of calm. His experiences in Vietnam—like those of so many thousands of soldiers—caused terrible PTSD and surely contributed to his later addiction. But in this small moment, my dad found comfort in his guitar and in music. And he shared this love with the other soldiers around him.

He was always musically inclined, though he never took lessons. He could hear a song on the radio and then, after just a few tries on the guitar, nail it. And he was always making up jazz or blues songs on cue, even without his guitar. Sometimes I'd say, "Hey, Dad, do you remember that one time..." And he'd burst into song, making up playful lyrics to capture that memory.

Sadly, I didn't get this gene. Reading music has always been like reading Greek to me. When my daughters started playing piano, I tried to learn along with them, but it just never clicked.

But for my dad, music was easy, joyful, and ever-present.

Dad in Vietnam

* * *

After I returned from the conference in San Francisco, I sent an email to both Dad and Max introducing them virtually.

Unfortunately, these emails have since been lost, but I recall clearly how each man responded. They both jumped into the conversation quickly, showing their distinct personalities.

My dad, always worried about the impression he made, was more cautious. Eager, yes, but also cautious, and he acknowledged the strangeness of the situation. It's interesting because he wasn't like this at AA meetings. I attended a few with him over the years, whenever I visited. In AA, he was looked up to and admired by the group—and that reflected on him. He radiated calm confidence and thoughtfulness in his speech. But around his peers, he was more energetic, unpredictable, and always having to bite his tongue.

In these early interactions with Max, Dad was worried about saying the wrong thing. He didn't want to leave a bad first impression, but he was also hesitant, feeling that he didn't know anything about this guy Max, after all, and that he ought to protect himself a bit.

Max, on the other hand, already had the advantage of a few week's worth of communication with me. His responses seemed totally at ease. I'm sure he was nervous, too, but his early emails expressed profound excitement. He couldn't wait to learn more about what they had in common. He was eager to start this new chapter in his life. His tone was so welcoming and friendly.

For the first couple of emails, I joined in. But it quickly became clear that they didn't need me to mediate. And it wasn't long—maybe just a week—before Dad and Max moved on to phone calls.

As it turned out, Dad and Max had even more in common than I'd first realized. I had learned from my correspondence with Max that they were both avid fishermen with full-on Boomer personalities. They worked hard, did the right thing, and thought the rest of the world was lazy. They loved their land, all things Americana, and being family men.

But they also had the same sense of humor. Dad and Max loved John Candy and Rodney Dangerfield. They bonded over their love of *Uncle Buck*, *Throw Mama from the Train*, and *Harry and the Hendersons*. And it's no wonder: they were both screwball comics with big and tender hearts.

And music was everything to Max, just like Dad. The son of a preacher, Max grew up in the ministry and from an early age had learned to play and perform on all kinds of musical instruments. He had converted a room in his Texas home into a recording studio and regularly gave lessons to students. Once upon a time, he had even toured with the Allman Brothers as a guitarist for one year and had produced his own gospel album.

As I was quickly learning, Max Frazier never went half-in with something. When he took on a project or decided to love someone, he went full-in and gave it his all. So when my dad turned sixty-one that April—just a few weeks after they'd been talking—Max sent him an unforgettable birthday gift.

And, since this was Max, he went above and beyond. He sent Dad a recording of "Happy Birthday," but he not only wrote new and original lyrics; he roped in several of his musical friends to help him play it. And, since this was Max, his musical friends were brilliant, highly accomplished musicians: Milo Deering (DoBro), Buddy Whitington (electric guitar), James DeLong (drums), David Long (piano), and George Anderson (bass guitar). With Max himself on guitar and vocals, the band was complete.

The song is upbeat and country. It makes you want to start dancing. Here are the lyrics:

"Happy Birthday, Day"
by Max Frazier

There was a man born in '48
He's alive and he's kickin' today
Lived most his life in Cali-forn-i-a
Ohhh Ohhhhhh, my brother Day!

A United States Marine and he fought in 'Nam
He lives in Placerville where it's quiet and calm
He climbs Half Dome when he wants to play
And he's a hero, they say, my brother Day

Well, it's your birthday, and you're sixty-one
And you still know how to have some fun
We've never met, but I have to say
I'm so proud to have my brother Day!

We never knew that each other existed
and in the sixties he enlisted
I hit the road and guitars I played
Someday I'm gonna meet my brother Day!

We gotta a lotta catchin' up to do
'cuz neither one of us is even close to through
Life's a lot, and we like to play
Ohhh Ohhhhhh, my brother Day!

Well it's your birthday, and you're sixty-one
And you still know how to have some fun
We've never met, but I have to say,
I'm so proud to have my brother Day!

Happy Birthday, Happy Birthday Day
Happy Birthday, Happy Birthday Day
Happy Birthday, Happy Birthday Day
Happy Birthday, Ohhhhhh Day

Dad was overwhelmed. No one in his family had ever done (or could ever do) anything remotely close to this.

* * *

From the moment I learned of Max's existence I'd been ready to hop on a plane to Texas.

But I decided to leave it to Max and Dad to determine what was right for them. After all, I'd been mulling over the existence of another, biological family since that first conversation with Grandma Gini when I was sixteen. But Max and Valerie had only just had this bomb dropped on them. I didn't want to be pushy.

Max was the one who brought it up first, suggesting a long weekend together. He offered to fly up with Valerie and their two grown children, Tania and Steven.

"No," I said. "There are only two of us. Dad and I will come to you and get a hotel."

"Okay," Max said, "but I'll insist that you all stay with us. We have plenty of room. We think you'll be comfortable."

Dad confirmed he was comfortable with it. To me, this spoke volumes to how well he felt he knew Max already and how natural the relationship felt to him.

Neither Dad nor I had ever been to Texas. When we stepped out of the Dallas-Fort Worth airport, August's heat and humidity practically assaulted us. It was unreal.

I could tell Dad was a little nervous, but before I had time to ask him about it, Max and Valerie were pulling up to the curb.

After the initial hugs and greetings and putting our luggage in the back, we piled in. Valerie moved to the back to sit with me and allow Dad to be up front with Max. I found this to be so thoughtful and welcoming of her.

Initially, it felt a little awkward in the car. We chatted about the flight and the weather and the freeway.

Then I noticed a 9mm handgun in the center console.

"Is that a gun, Max?" I asked him. I come from a family of gun owners. Both Joe and my dad are hunters and sportsmen, so I asked more out of curiosity and wanting to break the ice than out of any anxiety over the sight of it in the car.

"Yes, ma'am," he responded. "If you're in Texas and not carrying a gun, you're not a Texan!" We all chuckled.

The conversation soon shifted so that Dad and Max were chatting up front, while Valerie and I chatted in the back.

"I just saw this great movie the other night," Valerie offered. "With Richard Dreyfus, Holly Hunter, and John Goodman? But now I can't remember the name."

I felt a small thrill. "Do you mean *Always*?"

"Yes, that's it!"

"Oh my gosh," I said, "I love that movie. When Holly Hunter closes her eyes and asks Richard Dreyfus what color they are? I swoon every time."

"Yes!" Valerie said excitedly. "I did too."

I have no idea what the guys were talking about up front, but Valerie and I had connected quickly. She could have been hesitant about the meeting and bringing us into her home, but I sensed no apprehension. It was a long car ride, nearly an hour, so I was glad that any awkwardness had dissipated so quickly.

Their home in Azle was a beautiful one-story brick of fairly new construction. Max and Valerie showed us our rooms and gave us a quick tour of the house. It was a lovely home. My dad was thrilled to see the now-famous recording studio.

It would prove to be a packed weekend, but that first night, as at times throughout the weekend, we simply sat around and got to know each other. We noticed similarities that hadn't been obvious from photos. We all laughed because Dad and Max were sitting the same way, right leg crossed over left, leaning back. They both had small hands with stocky, pudgy fingers. And their blue eyes, face shape, and light, freckly skin complexion looked even more alike in person. We also noted their differences. Dad was a little taller, and Max was more of an out-loud laugher, like me. Dad tended to smile and nod, quietly appreciating the moment.

At one point that first night Max said to me, "When I look at your arms, I see my mother's."

That naturally led to us talking about their mother and wondering what had happened with the pregnancy and adoption. I fetched a packet of research that I'd stored away in my suitcase, which was filled with more photos and the original letters between Virginia Whitley and Grandma Gini. We passed them around. It was very moving to see Max holding and reading the letters from his young mother. It made me recall that day Grandma Gini had handed me the small stack that included them—how I held them so tightly, sensing the treasure trove within.

Valerie told me recently that she distinctly remembered pulling out a VHS tape of a home video to show us. I have no recollection of this moment, but she said we were all crying before the video was over. I can only imagine how powerful it must have been for my dad to see his mother's movements and mannerisms, to hear her voice.

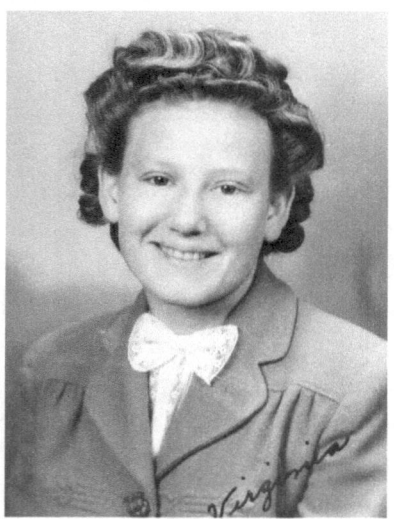

Virginia Whitley

We all wondered and discussed why she had given Dad up and who the father might have been. I shared my vision of the Fleet Week whirlwind romance.

"So Max," I asked, "you had no idea about any of this? No clue who the father might be?" I was so hopeful he might have been waiting to tell us something more in person.

Max shook his head. "None at all. I'm completely perplexed." He was thoughtful for a while. "You know, I've obviously been thinking about this a lot over the past couple of months. And I'm still so shocked. But at the same time, a lot now makes sense to me."

Max went on to describe his relationship with his mother. He never felt close to her. She wasn't especially affectionate, rarely hugging him, rarely expressing love.

"I've been reading about adoption lately too," Max went on, "and it's interesting. A lot of half siblings who are born after a child who was given up seem to have a similar experience of not feeling close to their mother. It's as if in giving up the first child, the mother is afraid to attach too much to the second.

"I was lucky, though, because I was really close to my dad. I never experienced any doubt about his love and affection. I think that's why this is all so puzzling. I can understand my mom never sharing her story with me. But after she passed away, why didn't my dad tell me? Is it possible she never told *him*? That feels unbelievable. But either way, someone was withholding the truth. My mother was lying to my father, or my father eventually lied to me."

My heart ached for Max. So much was now turned upside down for him.

It wasn't all heavy conversations, though. We played board games and toured around Fort Worth. We visited the Fort Worth Stockyards, and I was amazed at the size of Texas longhorns. Truly astonishing. We walked around town and stopped in a fun spice shop. At one point, Dad and Max went out on their own to check out a nearby fishing lake. Another day, they spent a long time in the studio together on guitars, just jamming and riffing off each other. My dad practically glowed with happiness.

Dad and Max in Fort Worth

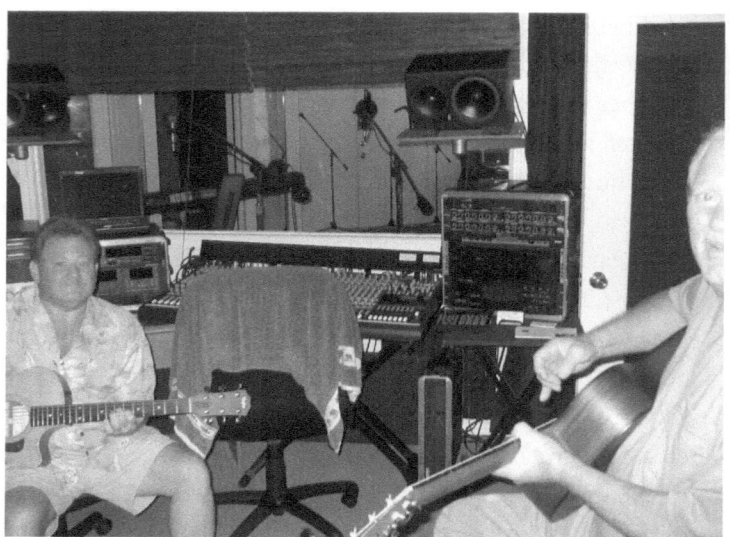

Dad and Max in the studio

Max and Valerie's daughter, Tania, lived nearby with her husband, Ricardo, and two daughters. They came over for dinner one of the nights, and another night we went to their home in Fort Worth. I had been nervous about meeting Tania. We had already connected over Facebook and email, but—as usual—I worried about making the wrong impression. The last thing I wanted was for her to think Dad and I had any ulterior motives

Tania is quiet, more on the reserved side, and a good listener. Unlike me, she's not at all a nervous talker, who feels the need to fill the air when there is a pause in conversation. At first it felt a little awkward with her because she wasn't offering much and I was probably offering too much, but now when we see each other, it's a lot easier. We did bond over talking about being girl moms, though, and I found her to be really kind and lovely.

Tania and me

Max and Valerie's son, Steven, had recently gone through a divorce and was living with them temporarily, but we didn't see much of him. He seemed to have a lot going on that weekend, and Max commented that he'd been having a hard time and probably wouldn't feel up to hanging out with us just yet. One of the nights, though, Dad and Max went out to dinner with him. Steven was also ex-military, and Max had been struggling to understand everything he'd been through. He thought Dad might be able to speak with him about dealing with PTSD and impart some wisdom and coping strategies.

We were there over a Sunday, and I had wondered whether Max and Valerie would want or expect us to go to church with them. I knew that might make my dad a little uncomfortable. But they didn't. We just spent more time together on Sunday, our last full day together.

I'd been waiting for a good opportunity to ask Max about his aunts, those mysterious sisters of Virginia. I'd been hitting so many walls at that point, and—like with my dad's biological father—I was holding out hope he might have some small key.

"I really don't know anything about them," he said, and my heart sank. "I remember a visit once from her sister Marjorie and her daughter. But I wasn't interested in playing with a girl, and I just went off and did my own thing."

Max recalled, "Another time, I remember that my mother received a cease and desist letter from one sister. I think she'd been trying to get back in touch with them. She was probably after money or something. But I don't know which sister that was."

Later, I asked Ernestine about the visit—and she remembered it too. It had made an impression on her because the Fraziers were living in an old funeral home at the time. But she knew nothing about the legal tension between the sisters. Neither did Imogene's daughter, Bonnie.

I asked more about Virginia Whitley's upbringing. What did Max know about it?

It was in this conversation with Max that I learned more about Virginia Whitley being placed in foster care, confirming what I'd read in the obituary from Monda. At the time, I'd been so overwhelmed by the information she gave me—not to mention excited by the sheer existence of Max—that I honestly hadn't paid much attention to the obit. I glazed over that detail of her being in foster care and did nothing with it.

"Mom went to live with a family named Corsaw," Max explained. "Harry and Hazel Corsaw. They had a son named Lyle, and his daughter, Sandra Corsaw Watts, actually lives in Hawaii—I have her address. Perhaps you could reach out to her to see if she knows more? It's possible, given the timing, that her father knew about Mom's pregnancy. And maybe he told her?"

(It'll probably come as no surprise that when I returned home, I immediately sent a letter to Sandra Corsaw Watts!)

Our visit wrapped up, and we all agreed how fun and wonderful our time had been together. It's amazing—looking back on that first visit—how there was never any tension. Awkwardness at first, of course, but never anything but positive warmth and goodwill. It all felt incredibly natural.

Dad invited them to visit him next in Placerville, and Max expressed his desire to meet Joe and our daughters.

"Something tells me I'm going to like Joe a lot."

"Oh, you will!" I laughed. "I definitely married my father."

Valerie, Max, Dad, and me

Despite the joys of that first meeting, I couldn't help but feel my own selfish twinge of disappointment. I desperately wanted to learn more about the Whitley family tree. And, other than the foster home information, Max knew next to nothing.

I was, however, beyond thrilled for my Dad to have connected with Max. After so many years, after their individual disappointments in their families, the growing brotherhood and love between them felt nothing short of miraculous. Following our trip to Texas, the brothers were in touch constantly. They visited each other a few times a year. They fished together frequently, and in each other they found a deep and beautiful, brotherly bond that they had only ever dreamed of.

I am now going to warn you about something, though. This story won't ultimately have a happy ending.

But for a while, for a good while—for years—it truly did.

Strong men!

KNOWING WHAT I KNOW NOW

When I learned that Virginia Whitley had gone on to have a life after giving my dad up for adoption, it had quite the humbling effect on me. I had thought I knew everything, and I was overconfident in my research abilities and assumptions.

So when I went to Texas, I felt more open. I was very conscious of not having expectations for who Max and Valerie might turn out to be. I only wish I'd been equally conscious of not having expectations for what Max would *know* about his family. His lack of knowledge about the Whitleys left me deeply disappointed. It never occurred to me that he wouldn't have more answers for me.

If someday you're able to meet your new family, don't be heartbroken if you don't get all the answers you're looking for. Sometimes you may learn new information that raises more questions than it answers. Max's knowledge of the Corsaw family, for instance, opened a new window of opportunity for me. They had been in no family tree or census I'd found. But what I would eventually discover in their family would change everything I thought I knew about Virginia Whitley's situation.

Consider bringing a binder with your research and other photos. Sometimes, with all the various emotions in such a meeting, you may forget details you'd hoped to inquire about. If the opportunity arises, then you can bring it out. But you may intuit that the first meeting isn't the best time for it. Trust your gut.

Try not to have your guard up and to have an open mind instead. Be willing to listen and to hold off on any assumptions and judgments. Just take it all in. Don't stereotype. We're all human, after all. We all have feelings and are just living our lives the best way we know how.

I felt some initial judgment toward the Fraziers' style of charismatic Christianity. Given our experience with my uncle Steve and his views, I was probably just nervous Max would prove to be similarly rigid. I had to consciously force myself to be open to their faith. But once I did, I discovered that their style was far more open and accepting than I'd expected.

But what if you're disappointed in something you observe about your family? What if something feels like an off-putting discovery? Just remember that this is *always true* in families. There will always be family members who walk to a different drum beat, have differing political views, or just annoy you. When you meet new family as an adult, it can prove harder to adjust to those differences.

But be patient. Give it time. Give people grace.

Chapter 8

BROTHERS

—

SHORTLY AFTER DAD AND I RETURNED FROM TEXAS, I wrote a letter to Sandra Corsaw Watts, the daughter of Virginia Whitley's foster brother, Lyle Corsaw.

Signing it jointly from Max and me, I explained how I was connected to the Fraziers and asked her if she had any information on Virginia that she might be able to share. I mailed it to the address in Hawaii that Max had given me.

Sandra wrote me back and confirmed that Virginia Whitley had lived with her grandparents when she was a young teenager. She was under their care until she married Max Frazier Sr. Her father was born in 1919, so eight years older than Virginia, making Sandra far too young to remember anything about her pregnancy with Day. She was, however, a flower girl in Virginia and Max Sr.'s wedding when she was five years old. She added that she faintly remembered something negative about Virginia's father but couldn't recall what it was. Since both Lyle and Sandra were only children and her mother had already passed away, there unfortunately wasn't anyone else around to ask. She wished Max and me well on our search for answers.

While I was grateful Sandra Corsaw Watts took the time to write back to me, it was certainly disappointing to hit *yet another* dead end.

* * *

Max and Valerie had been high school sweethearts.

He was completely smitten with her and wanted to marry her before anyone else could "discover what an angel she was." He proposed in high school, but her parents demanded that they wait until Valerie graduated. They waited, but just barely. Very soon after graduation, Max and Valerie married.

Max and Valerie, 1974

Max's father was a preacher, so he'd grown up in the church. Once married, Max and Valerie went on a lot of missions together: to the remotest areas of Alaska, to Mexico, to South Africa, and to Haiti. Their trip to Haiti in 2008 followed the devastating hurricane there, and they went down to help with relief efforts. At one point they found themselves at the center of a skirmish between relief workers and a local armed gang, who were trying to steal relief supplies. Max told us about how he and Valerie had had to flatten themselves on the ground as bullets whizzed menacingly above. Thank god nobody was injured.

They also started a company in Texas (the one with the PO box I'd originally written to!) that focused on managing missionary and humanitarian efforts: World Outreach Organization.

In 2013, Max and Valerie sold their house in Texas and moved into a fifth wheel, which they then took up to Colville, Washington. It's a small population on the Colville River—a tributary of the Columbia River. About halfway between Spokane and the Canadian border, the area is full of green hills and tall pine trees. It's cold and snowy in the winter and lushly green in the summer. Lots of hunters come through there during hunting season.

They wanted to be closer to Valerie's parents, who were declining. Initially, they lived on their church's property, but they soon moved to Valerie's parents' land, where they continued to live out of the fifth wheel.

During the harsh Colville winters, they moved down to an RV park in Arizona. Max being Max, he made himself useful and memorable wherever he went.

"You know," he said to the manager of the RV park, "if you comp our rent, I could help run your recreation area—keep your sound system going and even put on a Sunday worship service." So just like that, Max simultaneously struck a deal and became indispensable to the RV park.

He and Valerie had a huge dog—mastiff huge—named Annabelle, but Max didn't like walking her. When she stood up, she was over six feet tall. So he'd hop in the park's golf cart, hook her leash to it, and drive her around for her daily walks. Annabelle happily trotted alongside him, tongue swinging. People would come out of their RVs and chuckle at the sight of this guy in his golf cart driving around the massive dog. Children adored Annabelle and were always coming up to ask to give her pets. Max loved it.

By 2017, both Valerie's parents had passed, and she and Max decided to stay put in Colville and Addy for good. They moved into a house on the church property and were (of course!) of service to all things with the church. Max helped with all the musical equipment and sound systems. Valerie helped with office duties, childcare, and other church affairs. They mentored new parishioners and were an integral part of this small community—well liked and adored by all.

* * *

Over the years, Dad and Max would see each other frequently. At least a few times a year, they'd get together to fish, shoot, or play music. Dad would head up to visit them in Addy and stay several days, and then he'd pop over to Idaho to visit his AA sponsor, Skip, and Skip's wife, Melanie. Or he'd visit Max and Valerie in Arizona depending on the season.

Wherever they were—Texas, California, Washington, or Arizona—it was like Dad and Max were making up for lost time. They enjoyed each other's corny jokes, made up song lyrics, and riffed on each other. They absolutely cracked each other up. They really were meant to be brothers.

One of Dad and Max's favorite places to fish became a spot just outside Spokane: Big Meadow Lake. It's a relatively shallow lake filled with rainbow trout and surrounded by mountains and deep-green, dense Washington pine forest. It's a truly peaceful and gorgeous place.

They both loved the outdoors and simply being in nature.

My dad was actually a big-time mountain man, hiker, and wilderness camper. Whenever someone hadn't seen him for a while, they'd always ask, *What mountain have you climbed lately, Day?* Then, of course, he'd launch into a story about his latest hiking adventure, the big bear he'd seen, how he pissed his daughter off because he went off the trail without telling the rangers, and so forth.

Dad and me hiking in El Dorado

It was true. He was always driving me nuts. He'd set off on a solo ten-day trek and do everything he was supposed to, submitting his well-thought-out plan to the rangers. In case he didn't return on time, they'd be able to track where he'd been and send out a rescue team.

But then—inevitably—five hours in, my fearless dad would change his mind and veer off course. He never checked with either the rangers or me, and I wouldn't learn about his impromptu new trek until he'd returned.

"Oh my god, Dad!" I'd always groan. "You're going to get eaten by a mountain lion, and I'll never find your body!"

I could practically hear him rolling his eyes through the phone. He never changed his ways.

He had retired from carpentry by this time, but he often helped people out with small building projects. Someone was always asking for his help with a deck or a fence. He was still participating regularly in AA and NA meetings. Sometimes he would just be an attendee, but he was so beloved and admired he mostly chaired them. He still volunteered at the Progress House in Coloma.

Max would visit him at his house in Placerville. The idea of these two big, burly outdoorsmen in that little house always struck me as funny. It's a sweet, yellow, gingerbread house, built in the 1930s. My dad had placed bright sunflower-patterned curtains in the front windows that could be seen from the road.

When Max visited, my dad always took him to his favorite fishing lakes: Icehouse, Silver Lake Chapels, and Red. They never went hiking together, though, as that wasn't something Max enjoyed, but Dad would take Max and Valerie for drives around beautiful, winding Northern California and through the Sierras. He often took them to his favorite restaurants: Smith Flat House and Bricks Eats & Drinks.

Sometimes in the fall Joe, the girls, and I would join the three of them for festivals and lunches at Abel's Apple Acres or Apple Hill. While the girls played in the corn mazes, we would talk over a picnic. We always bought apple pies to have for dessert—and frozen ones to bring home later.

All of us in Placerville after spending the day at Apple Hill, 2014.

* * *

But life will be life, so not all of our times together were centered on pleasure and adventure.

In 2012, Max and Valerie's son, Steven, passed away unexpectedly. We were devastated for them. Dad had often offered advice to help Max and Valerie, as Steven struggled with the aftereffects of military combat and a divorce: two experiences Dad understood intimately but Max didn't.

We went back down to Texas for the funeral. At the service, Dad spoke about the challenges of being ex-military and going through war times. How a man had to be both tough *and* tender. On one hand, he is the tough military man—fighting for his country, for his platoon, and for his way of life so that he can protect his family. But on the other hand, he is the tender man who loves his wife and children and wants to be a husband and father at home—who is no longer at war. He spoke about how these two men often became entangled. How the military man found himself at war with the husband and father role, unable to reconcile each persona in a way that would create a peace for the soul in order to properly function in a home. I think Dad felt the need to describe this tough and tender heart dilemma to the funeral attendees, especially if they had never experienced military combat. I also think that Dad understood Steven intimately in one particular way that his parents—having neither been in combat and nor been through a divorce—simply couldn't. The aftereffects of both experiences run deep, and Dad had offered advice to help Max and Valerie over the years.

After the funeral, Dad stayed on for a few days.

* * *

Dad and Max's profound brotherhood—which developed almost instantly—was unexpected for them both. But they also recognized how much they had both yearned for it.

My dad, with his distant and often fraught relationship with his brother, Steve Horner, had experienced nothing like this kind of recognition and intimacy. And all the ways he'd felt different growing up—his sense of humor, his love of music, his easy, nonjudgemental helpfulness to those around him—were reflected in Max. For the first time, I think Dad didn't feel lonely. There was now someone else in the world who saw things the same way he did, who saw him for who he was and truly loved him for it. And even in the ways he differed most from Max—his years of addiction and his nonbelief in God—were never judged by Max. He took him as he was and never judged him for it or tried to change him.

And for Max, the relationship was just as powerful. "I had no idea," he said once, "that this was missing from my life. But now that you're here, Day, I realize how much I needed and wanted this."

I think the discovery of Max's family secret also helped him to finally understand and forgive his mother. Virginia Whitley Frazier found Max hard to love. According to Max, as she aged, she became a bitter, angry woman who was often sickly, struggling with diabetes and asthma. But once he took in what she'd been through in her youth and how she must have always carried regret and disappointment over having to give her first son away, it helped Max to come to terms with why she had mothered him the way she had. Maybe she would have been this way anyway—there's no way to truly know, of course—but the knowledge was healing to Max regardless.

KNOWING WHAT I KNOW NOW

I had to learn how to leave Dad and Max alone.

I was not in the primary relationship—I was a bystander. And sometimes I found that frustrating. As they built their relationship, I had to learn how to have patience with their pace. Especially in the beginning, I wanted for them to move faster, call more often, meet up more frequently. But I needed to just leave them alone and let their relationship evolve as it would. But overall, it did move quite quickly.

I wanted a relationship with Max, too, of course. And we built that over time. He was a truly wonderful uncle to me.

If you're a bystander, as I was, try to have patience. Never force a fit. If you let things progress organically, the relationship will have a much greater chance of survival. But also approach the relationship with curiosity. Does it need encouragement? If you sense hesitance or anxiety in either party, why? Ask questions and listen.

If you, like Dad or Max, are an actual participant in the relationship, try also to have patience. The other person may not want to move as quickly or as slowly as you do. That's okay. Don't take personal offense if they're on a different timeline.

We were lucky because the relationship between Dad and Max moved quickly and lovingly. But a new sibling relationship is generally less complicated than a parent-child.

Chapter 9

CODA

———

ONE DAY UP IN WASHINGTON, MAX WAS CHOPPING wood when a small chunk flew off a log and gashed his shin. It was summer, and he'd been wearing shorts. The cut bled a while, but it was only a couple of inches long, and Max didn't think more of it.

A week later, I called him, as I regularly did. "How are things going up there in Washington?"

"Oh, pretty good," he said. We spoke about what he and Valerie had been up to, the weather, their church, about Dad's most recent visit, and possibly planning the next.

And then he said, "But you know, I've got this cut on my shin from chopping wood. And it just doesn't seem to want to heal." He described it in detail, and it sounded like more than just a scratch.

"That's not good, Max. It's probably infected."

"Yeah, maybe. It's really red now."

"Will you send me a picture?" Because Max tended to underplay anything medical, I was surprised—and a little concerned. If he was bothering to mention it to me, then that meant it wasn't nothing.

"Uh, sure. Okay. Hold on."

Several seconds later, my phone dinged and I stared at a picture of Max's leg. It didn't look as bad as I feared, but it definitely wasn't good. The scratch was about the length of my thumb, and the skin around it was really irritated. More than irritated, really. It looked pissed off.

I started harping on him. Had he used Neosporin? Hydrogen peroxide? I listed all my "mom" remedies for cuts. By now, Max genuinely felt like the close family he was. I was comfortable talking to him just like I did to Dad.

"Yeah, yeah," he said. It sounded like he'd tried everything but nothing was working.

"Then you might need antibiotics." I was sure Valerie had given him the same advice, but Max, like his brother, could be super—*frustratingly*—stubborn when it came to doctors. I said it anyway. "You need to go to a doctor, Max."

"Yeah, maybe I will." He sounded about as noncommittal as a person could.

* * *

A few weeks later, the wound had grown a lot worse. Max relented and finally saw a doctor. He came home with a cream and oral antibiotics and a recommendation to come back in a week if the wound still wasn't better.

Over the next several months Max would be in and out of doctors' offices. The wound was getting worse and obviously had become super infected. They prescribed more creams, more antibiotics. They tried wrapping the leg tightly. But the wound became gangrenous. Nothing worked. Doctors were baffled. And all the while, Max was in pain! He and Valerie were dumbfounded that the doctors couldn't make this thing heal.

Then, by December, the infection had spread to both legs. Valerie was now taking him to dermatologists, hematologists, infectious disease experts, and rheumatologists. Finally, they thought they had somewhat good news: an accurate diagnosis. But it turned out that pyoderma gangrenosum was a rare autoimmune disorder—and there simply wasn't a lot of research in it. And trying to find a specialist was challenging, especially in northern Washington.

Over the next year, Max continued to be in and out of hospitals, sometimes for monthlong stays. His wounds grew deeper—so deep that his tendons and muscles were exposed. He battled sepsis off and on. Valerie and Tania started a GoFundMe to help pay for the growing medical expenses and were overwhelmed by the outpouring of support. But, unfortunately, things just did not improve medically for Max. His legs became so eaten away by the pyoderma gangrenosum that he was faced with what seemed to be the only option: a double leg amputation. It was that the disease could continue to spread up his legs and to the rest of his body. And while he and Valerie had hoped for below-the-knee amputation, it just wasn't possible.

During all these challenging months, in and out of ERs and hospitals and in and out of stretches of hope, Valerie was Max's main caregiver. She was his angel, changing his painful wound dressings daily, consulting with doctors, and pushing him to keep getting better. They were a good team.

By that time, Tania, Ricardo, and their girls had left Fort Worth, and after living in Peru for a period, they had settled in Georgia. Tania visited her parents as much as she could, but frequent visits to Washington just weren't possible.

From the start, Max and Valerie received a lot of support from their church community. Meal trains, social visits, any supplies they needed, the community rallied around the Fraziers. They built a wheelchair ramp up to the house. So many community efforts got him the resources he needed. Pastor Tim would bring church to him on Sundays when he couldn't attend in person, so they were able to praise when they needed to praise. Overall, there was just incredible community support.

Additionally, Jana, their son Steven's ex-wife, was a nurse in nearby Spokane. Max really loved her. Once a week she would come to their home and be a caretaker so Valerie could go into town or all the way into Spokane.

My dad helped out, too, as much as he could from California. He helped to purchase Max an electric wheelchair and stayed in touch frequently with phone calls and visits to Washington.

It was really hard on him, watching Max's drawn-out demise. He would occasionally say things to me like, "If this ever happens to me, Jennifer, please just shoot me." Or sometimes, "If I was faced with what he's faced with, I'd jump off Half Dome."

I'm sure Max felt that way at some points too. But until any of us are actually faced with such a situation, it's impossible to know exactly how we'll feel or react. Max fought the whole way.

Despite my dad's fear, as a man, of being incapacitated, Max's suffering also inspired him.

The arrival of COVID-19 hadn't been good for Dad. Isolation is never good for someone in recovery. Many people became first-time alcoholics during the mandated COVID-19 lockdowns, and many addicts relapsed. But Dad was very lucky—he was able to stay sober. He did, however, stop going to the gym. So he gained weight and lost a lot of mobility. He also lost his tight-knit AA community that had been so critical for his mental health over the years. His political views grew stronger and more extreme, and he complained about everything. It felt like he was becoming an angry, old Republican.

It wasn't long, though, before his tune started changing. "I really need to suck it up and stop being a baby," he'd say. "Look what Max is going through. My brother has no legs, and I'm complaining about not going to the gym."

After Max's double amputation, his medical team kept checking the amputation areas for any recurring spots of pyoderma gangrenosum. Technically, it was still in his body, like cancer or a virus, but its potential harm depended on whether his cells would reactivate it. He was taking monoclonal antibodies (MABs) as a targeted drug therapy, as well as Remicade, and it seemed to be working. The infection didn't appear to be returning.

But Max, living as a double amputee, was in constant pain, and the last two and a half years had taken an enormous toll on his body. To say the least, none of the trauma had served his diabetes or cardiovascular health well.

* * *

In May of 2022, Dad and I spent several wonderful days in Washington, visiting Max and Valerie.

One evening, I cooked a spaghetti and french bread dinner for them, one of Joe's mom's famous Wallig recipes. I was happy to let Valerie relax in the living room with Dad and Max while I cooked in the kitchen. The french bread didn't come out like it was supposed to, but we all laughed and ate it anyway.

Later that evening, we belatedly celebrated Dad's birthday. Max was in his hospital bed in their living room, drowsy from pain meds, in and out of consciousness, when Valerie brought out a cake.

"Are we going to sing 'Happy Birthday'?" she asked the room.

"Yes, of course!" Max declared, surprising us all. Dad and I looked at each other and smiled. He was still there.

Suddenly, Max burst into song. But instead of the familiar first few notes of "Happy Birthday," Max sang "Tiny Bubbles."

Dad joined in, and we all started laughing. Next we sang "Happy Birthday," and then, for good measure, followed it up with "New York, New York." Annabelle the dog joined in too.

It was such a beautiful, silly, happy evening. And yet we also knew it might be one of our last with Max. Did that make it happier? Did the impending sadness make us laugh a little harder, embrace the silliness a little tighter? All I know for sure is that I'll forever be grateful for that memory. Max and Dad were two dorky and silly peas in a pod. And neither illness nor pain could dampen the life they gave to each other.

During that visit, Dad and I stayed at a nearby lodge to give Max and Valerie a little more space and privacy. Dad had been having issues for years with circulation in his legs, but lately it seemed to be getting worse. He would go for walks and his calves would knot up, causing him a lot of pain. One evening, back at the lodge, we were watching TV, and I was harping on him to get his unusually bloated and blue veins checked out.

"You're going to lose a foot!" I told him. "You need to do something about it."

He just scoffed. But I really worried about him. I climbed into his bed and snuggled up to him.

"I love you, Dad."

"What are you doing? Leave me alone!" He huffed, all macho-like.

"I'm cuddling with you, Dad," I said. "Just get over it."

"Okay, my beautiful daughter."

* * *

Later that year, in September, Max returned yet again to the hospital.

Valerie and Tania kept in touch over the next few weeks to let us know what was going on. It didn't sound good. Dad was really worried, and when we would talk on the phone he'd say, "I think my brother might die, Jennifer."

I wanted to console my father and tell him not to worry, that it would all be fine. But I was scared too. I feared it wouldn't end well. Every time I talked to Valerie on the phone, I died a little more inside. How do you talk to a woman whose husband has been in and out of hospitals, been eaten away by some crazy rare disease, lost both his legs, and now things were not good, not good at all? I was scared. Dad was scared. And our hearts ached so much for Valerie and Tania.

On October 1, Valerie called me to say that he'd taken a turn for the worse. The doctors didn't think he was going to make it. She invited Dad and me to come up for a last visit.

"He'll be sedated," she said. "But he'll know you're there. Tania's on her way. She'll arrive tomorrow." Tania had to come all the way from Georgia. I remember praying that she would arrive in time. The idea that she might not make it to be with Max in time distressed me a lot.

I thanked her and told her we could be there immediately too. I'd just talk to Dad first.

"I can't do it," Dad said when I called him.

"This might be your last chance," I pleaded. I thought I understood his feelings, but I felt protective of him too. What if he was making an impulsive decision that he'd later regret?

But he was adamant. "I want May to be my last memory."

I didn't feel right going up without him—Max was his brother, after all. So I let Valerie know that Dad wasn't comfortable and we felt it should just be Tania and her at the end. She was very gracious.

That night, I lay in bed next to Joe and felt enormous guilt. I thought about what Valerie would suffer that night. How did it feel to know that every hour or minute might be the last you'd ever have again with this person you'd loved for years and years, the person you'd raised children with? I thought about Tania holding her father's hand the next day, watching him pass in a hospital, surrounded by sterility and machines. I don't think I slept very much that night.

When I hadn't heard from Valerie by October 3, I called. I hadn't texted or called before because I didn't want to interrupt or add any stress to the situation in the hospital room. More than anything, I just wished them peace.

"Oh, I'm so sorry, Jennifer," Valerie said when she picked up the phone. She sounded beyond fried. "I didn't call you, did I? It happened yesterday at the hospital." She told me Tania, Jana, Valerie's brother Gregg, and a lot of friends from their church were at the house helping her out. Tania *did make it* in time and was able to have some alone time with her father. I was relieved to hear that, at least.

I hung up with Valerie and started crying. Joe held me for some time. "This is just not fair!" I kept saying over and over through the tears. I just couldn't wrap my head around how such a good man could go through such bad things and how a good family could be subjected to a horrific death of their loved one. It was just not fair.

And now I had to call my dad.

I gathered myself together, picked up the phone, and called him. As his phone rang, I thought about how I'd had to tell him over the phone that his mother had died. And then again that I'd found his birth mother, but she had died too. And now I was about to tell him his brother had died. *At least*, I thought, *he's more prepared this time*. I wondered if he dreaded answering the phone when he saw it was me.

"I'm glad I wasn't there," he said, after we'd spoken about it. "I feel like I would have just been in the way." I didn't feel like we would have been in the way if we'd had gone, but I didn't tell Dad that. I just listened and acknowledged his feelings. In such a situation, there aren't any wrong feelings, after all. They were *his* feelings, even if I didn't share them. He cried. I cried. I told him I loved him so much and couldn't wait to see him again. He said the same.

After we hung up, I texted Dad's girlfriend, Cathey, to ask her to go over and be with him. I hated that we lived two hours away from each other.

* * *

They held the funeral in mid-November. It can get really snowy up there by then, but Valerie didn't want to wait till spring, and the roads were still drivable.

Dad and I flew in and stayed at the same hunting lodge. We spent the day before the funeral with Valerie, Tania, Ricardo, and Jana.

Tania and Ricardo's daughters were there, too, of course, and all grown up now. As well as Steven and Jana's two sons. We hadn't seen them in years. Dad delighted in telling them jokes.

"Oh, you're *that* guy!" Max's grandchildren laughed. "We remembered that joke, but not where it came from."

Thinking ahead to the funeral worried me a little. Dad and I lean toward the skeptical when it comes to organized religion, particularly Christianity. I'd never really had a positive experience before. And, besides, within our family we'd already had so much judgment from so-called Christians that walking into Summit Valley Community Church the next day for the funeral had filled me with a mild dread. What would the community be like? I loved the Fraziers, of course, but would I feel like an outsider? Would I be *made to feel* like an outsider? How would Dad feel about it? He was always joking that of course, he believed in a higher power—aliens.

But before I could worry further, the service began.

The funeral was beautiful. It was perfect. Valerie and Tania had put so much care into the program. They played some of Max's recorded songs, including his favorite, "I'll Fly Away." It was heartbreaking and lovely.

At one point, people got to stand up and reflect on Max. I knew Dad wanted to stand up and say something, but despite his years of doing exactly that in AA, he remained doubtful of his speaking abilities. It was like he had ten thoughts running around his mind at once, and he couldn't grab the one that he actually wanted to say. Sometimes people got frustrated with him. I noticed he was fidgety, and I put a hand on his knee.

"Are you sure?" I whispered when someone handed him the mic.

"Yep, I'm sure," he said and stood up.

After a couple of breaths, he began. "I never knew I had a brother until my daughter found him, and it was the best thirteen years of my life." He went on to describe the strong bond that he and Max shared and the challenges of watching such a strong man go through so much pain and torture. He acknowledged all Valerie had been through over the past three years and how much he admired her strength too. I tried not to cry while my dad was speaking. It was so hard to watch this strong man, whom I adore, suffer that much pain. I was glad that he was able to verbalize his feelings and say goodbye in his way.

After the funeral was over, several people came up to me, unexpectedly. They'd heard so much about Day and Jennifer, and were so glad to meet us finally. *Oh no*, I thought. *Are they going to investigate how Christian we are—or aren't?* But they truly couldn't have been warmer or nicer. They were amazed at the story of how I found Max and wanted to hear more. At one point, someone said, "You know, you really should write a book about this." Everyone was so complimentary, but I remember feeling very shy from all the attention and—despite their kindness—just wanting to recede into the background.

Eventually, I was able to find a quiet spot to sit by myself for a moment. I felt mentally exhausted.

After a little while, I heard someone approaching and looked up. It was Ricardo. He smiled at me and asked if he could join me.

"Of course." I smiled back. I love chatting with him. He's so kind and interesting, just a wonderful guy.

He pulled up a chair and said, "I just want to explain our church to you."

Oh no, really? I thought. *Ugh, not church talk.*

But instead of preaching to me or trying to convert me, as I'd somewhat feared, Ricardo did exactly what he said he would do. He simply explained their church to me.

"We're here because we want to be," he said. He went on to describe how many Christian churches are either very rigid—or very loose—in their approach to building a community. But Summit Valley Community Church and their church back in Georgia believed that God was in everyone, in every second and every detail of life. As Ricardo spoke, I found myself comforted and put at ease. Here was the first explanation of organized Christianity that felt in alignment with my own way of seeing the world. It was refreshing and actually made me want to become a part of their community. For the first time, I saw that perhaps there might actually be places that I wouldn't feel—or be made to feel—like an outsider.

I asked Ricardo questions and pushed him a little on some ideas. I felt comfortable enough to banter back and forth with him. I thanked him for coming over to me.

"I just didn't want to scare you off by how we have a relationship with God," he said.

"You haven't at all," I assured him. I felt a little overwhelmed by the conversation and by the day. But I was grateful to him. More than I could put into words. I will remember that conversation for the rest of my life.

Dad and I flew home a couple of days later. Exhausted, missing Max, and glad for our days in his community.

* * *

A couple of weeks later was Thanksgiving. Every year we spend it with my dad, but that year, Joe and I had planned to take an RV trip to Zion, the Grand Canyon, and Route 66, just the two of us. But given all that had happened recently, I was a bundle of nerves. I didn't want to spend a holiday away from Dad and my girls, even though my dad assured me that he and Cathey had awesome plans. My girls assured me they were honestly excited to not spend another boring holiday with the same old turkey, the same old games, and the same old jokes. They had plans with friends and were already creating their own Friendsgiving. Everyone but me wanted us to just go on our road trip and enjoy it. Looking back now, even though I was a stress-case most of the time, it was a beautiful trip. Joe and I saw some spectacular landscapes, did some low-key hiking, and rode e-bikes through the mountains. Our Thanksgiving meals were Hungry-Man microwave turkey dinners. And, plus, just having that time with my husband was priceless.

Because of the wake-up call that Max's death had been, Dad was better about getting outside and back to the activities he loved. Hiking and nature gave him natural highs and after so many months of being isolated and sedentary, he started going on short hikes again.

But unfortunately he was still experiencing numbness in his calves on some of those hikes. He finally went to a doctor, who told him he had blood flow issues in his lower legs and recommended vein bypass surgery. He brought it up at Christmas, when we were all together. We told him he should do it. He should get his mobility back and be healthy. I think all of us gathered around the table, the pain of his brother's absence, and how *he'd lost his legs* sparked something in my dad. He realized he didn't want to shorten his life any longer. He wanted to live and to be with his family.

I spent Valentine's Day with him in the hospital. The surgery went well, and Dad got good blood flow back into his calf and foot. But he got impatient during the two-month recovery. On one of the times I visited, he refused to use a cane as we walked down Main Street in Placerville. He was wobbly, and I was so scared he was going to take a tumble. So I just pretended that I wanted to hold his hand like when I was a little girl, but really I was stabilizing him.

By now, I was making the two-hour drive to Placerville all the time. For the past year, I'd sensed something was off with him, so I was spending a lot more time with him than usual. I'd just go up for the day.

"I can't believe you spend four hours on the road," he'd say, "just to spend four hours with me."

I'd shake my head. "But you're the only dad I have. Do you not want me to come?"

"No, I do."

"Then shut up. I'm going to keep coming."

By mid-March, Dad said he was starting to feel a lot better. He signed up for a gym membership. He started taking vitamins again. He made a weight-loss goal for his seventy-fifth birthday in April.

He spent Easter with our family, and I noticed he seemed to be doing better with walking steadily.

But of course, I worried about him. For some reason, my concern had been growing over the past year.

Because of this underlying worry that I had, I asked my dad if I could install a Ring doorbell at his house, and on his birthday, April 20, I looked into the doorbell videos for that morning before I called him to say happy birthday. There he was at the bottom of the back door stairs, leading from his driveway up to the mudroom. He was just standing there, one hand on each railing, looking up at the stairs. I wondered if the video had frozen, but then I noticed his chest gently heaving, like he was breathing hard. He'd climbed Half Dome many times. And now the prospect of a few stairs stopped him?

I didn't call him right away because I didn't want him to think I was stalking his Ring camera, so a few hours later, I gave him a call.

"Happy birthday, Dad!" I tried to sound more upbeat than concerned.

"Well, thank you." He didn't sound good.

"Are you okay?" I asked. "Are you sick?"

"Yeah, it's a little hard to breathe," he wheezed.

I told him to go to the doctor. But he didn't. Not that day, or the next, or the next. I spoke to him everyday, encouraging him to go. But he made it sound like it was fine, just a cold, just a chest thing, and not a big deal. But again, I was worried. I insisted, "Just go, Dad, please!"

By April 23, he couldn't breathe. He called Cathey in the middle of the night and asked her to take him to the ER.

It turned out he had COVID-19.

In general, Placerville is less alarmist about COVID-19 than, say, San Francisco. But still, the hospital he was in actually hadn't seen a case in some time. They isolated him in a glass room with an air filtration system that led directly outside. Nurses suited up in gowns, gloves, masks, and face shields before entering his room through a trapdoor.

When I visited, we FaceTimed through the glass. Teaching your seventy-five-year-old, sick, luddite father how to use an iPad by yelling through a glass wall between the two of you is *oh so much fun*.

But the nurses, doctors, and staff were all amazing. He received amazing care. He might have anyway, but I did my part to make sure. I always brought the nurses coffee and sweets when I visited. I thanked them profusely for taking care of him. I let them know how loved he was.

One of the nurses was particularly kind. She saw how difficult it was for me to be on the other side of the glass. There were only two other patients in the ICU then, so she looked around and said, "I didn't know you were a nurse, Jennifer." Her eyes were sparklingly mischievously.

I immediately got what she was doing. "Um, yeah," I smiled. "I do have a little training."

So she helped get me suited up so I could sit with him inside the room. We had a whole hour together, and it was wonderful.

In the hospital with Dad

I spent so many hours in that hospital that I joined a program called Caring Crochet. They took donated crochet items that they would then distribute to patients in hospice or undergoing cancer treatment. I finished one blanket and asked a nurse if she'd like to donate it directly to a patient in their hospital.

"No, honey," she said, holding up my small, dainty, light blue blanket. "This is going to your dad."

"Yeah," I said, "he's not going to want that. He's just going to throw it away and not care about it. It should go to someone who would like it." My dad didn't like extra items. He had low-key OCD and needed everything in its place and sorted perfectly. To add even a small blanket to his mix would upset his apple cart. It didn't bother me in the least, but the nurse wasn't having it.

She insisted. "We're going to make him care." She brought it to him, and I watched the interaction through the glass. He looked out at me with raised eyebrows, mouthing, "Seriously? This girly thing?"

But the nurse was right. By that night, he was wearing it around his neck like a scarf.

The blanket

After two weeks, Dad stopped testing positive for COVID-19, so they moved him out of solitary confinement and into the main ICU area. He developed bacterial pneumonia and was responding well to antibiotics, but still needed to be in the ICU. He was somewhat better, but they wanted to keep an eye on him a little longer. He looked so frail and weak to me. But leaving isolation was hopeful. I continued to make my trips to visit him in the hospital nearly every other day. I would leave work early in the Bay Area, make the two-hour drive, spend a few hours with him in the ICU, and then drive back home.

For the first few days out of solitary, things seemed to be looking up. I thought, *Great, he'll be home in a few days!* Then, almost overnight, things went south. His blood pressure skyrocketed. X-rays showed how compromised his lungs had become. The doctors said his lungs were showing scarring and the x-rays were so dark that I didn't understand. How could he be getting better but the x-rays were showing such bad lungs? They couldn't get him stabilized.

In the first week of May, one of his doctors told me that if things didn't improve, he'd need to go on a ventilator. In the back of my mind, I knew the ventilator was a death sentence. Nobody ever came off a ventilator. How could this be the only option to get him the oxygen he needed to live?

I turned to Joe, who was visiting then, too, and asked him to go home and get our girls. I wanted them to be able to see their grandpa before the ventilator. Something in me told me not to delay it.

Joe drove the four hours round trip, bringing the girls so they could have their time with their grandpa. It was so sweet, really. Even in his condition, Dad couldn't help joking around with them, making them laugh. And, of course, always the prankster, he pulled aside his gown at one point, flashing his hairy chest. "Grandpa boob!" he declared. The girls groaned and giggled.

But once they left, his whole demeanor changed. He looked exhausted and frail once again.

"Jennifer, I don't want you to tell anyone about this," he said. "No friends, no Facebook, please."

"Okay," I said. I could feel a knot welling up in my chest. He watched me watching him. I could tell he knew what was happening.

"And I need you to make me a deal," he went on. He was breathing hard.

I took his hand. "Anything, Dad."

"I don't want to die on the ventilator. But I don't want...the idea of waking up on it and..." he trailed off. I waited for him to catch his breath. "Just promise me you'll leave me on the thing for three days before you pull the plug."

The knot in my chest had reached my throat. I couldn't speak. I just nodded. He squeezed my hand.

The next day, they put him on the ventilator.

And the next day, his doctor told me, "He may not last the day."

I think my knees buckled, and somebody got me a chair before I crumbled to the floor. I was sobbing. "But I promised him three days—and I can't let him die on it."

The doctor nodded compassionately. "I can't guarantee he's going to make it that long. If you don't want him to die on the ventilator, I think it's time to take him off it." I went round and round with the doctor for quite a while, asking "what ifs" and about any other possible options. But it always came back to the same answer. I didn't want to make this choice. How could we be here? How was this happening?

I called Joe and told him to hurry back to the hospital. "Drive fast," I told him. "It's happening."

I invited Cathey to join me in the room with Dad. Despite my stress and shock, I thought about how unusual that invitation was for me. I was always so possessive of my dad. I hated sharing him with his girlfriends. But Cathey was different. *This* was different. For her own reasons, though, she decided to stay in the waiting room.

I asked the nurses to turn off all the noises. I didn't want to hear the beeping any longer. I didn't want to hear a flatline. I wondered, briefly, how I would know when it was over. Where was the instruction manual for this part of life?

When the nurse brought me into his room, I saw that they'd removed most of the wires and tubes. They'd cleaned him up nicely. He looked peaceful. I hated that I'd broken my promise to him. But he would not die with a tube down his throat. At least that I could do for him.

And then, as if reading my mind, the nurse placed a hand on my back and said, "You're doing the right thing for your father."

I sucked in air. "Thank you. I really appreciate that."

And then she left the room, and we were alone.

I sat beside him and held his hand and cried. It all felt so weird, and I didn't know what to do. I was alone.

So I started singing his favorite song, David Lee Roth's cover of "Just a Gigolo."[3] He himself had sung this song just a few days earlier to me and Joe. Then I got to the lines "There will come a day, when youth will pass away, do de doop, what will they say

---

[3] JUST A GIGOLO
Words and Music by IRVING CAESAR, JULIUS BRAMMER and LEONELLO CASUCCI
© 1930 (Renewed) IRVING CAESAR MUSIC CORP. and CHAPPELL & CO., INC.
All rights for IRVING CAESAR MUSIC CORP. Administered by WB MUSIC CORP.
All Rights Reserved.
Used by Permission of ALFRED MUSIC

about me? When the end comes, I know, it was just a gigolo, Life goes on...without me." And I started sobbing.

"Seriously, Jennifer?" I could almost hear Dad saying. "I'm lying here dying and *that's what you're singing to me?*"

I laughed out loud through the tears and snot flowing down my face. I knew he would have joined in singing next. I thought of us all singing around Max in his hospital bed, the silliness of it, the ache behind it. But I kept singing, "I ain't got nobody, nobody cares for me, nobody...I'm so sad and lonely...won't some sweet mama come and take a chance with me, cuz I ain't so bad." I had so many fond memories of my dad singing that song to me, and now I was singing it to him for the last time.

I wondered how long I'd been with him. Ten minutes? Forty minutes? I had no sense of time. Where was Joe?

And then I felt something shift. I said, "Okay, Max, you can take him now." I looked up toward the ceiling while squeezing my dad's hand tighter.

And I lingered at his bedside, holding his hand, stroking his arm. I don't know how long. Time had stopped.

Eventually, I pressed the red button to call the nurse.

She came in, and I didn't know what to say. She checked his vitals and the monitor. "He passed at 5:55 p.m.," she said gently.

I looked at the clock. That'd been a while ago, right around the time I spoke to Max, I guessed.

"Oh, okay," I said. And I sobbed and sobbed. I felt like collapsing on the floor. I managed to ask, "Can you please go see if my husband is here yet?"

She checked and Joe was just walking into the waiting room. The two of us stayed with Dad a little longer, and then Joe went to get Cathey.

* * *

On the way home, I stopped and bought gallons of ice cream. I hadn't called the girls yet. I was sure they sensed it, but I wanted to tell them in person.

It was late when I got home, past their usual bedtimes, but they were waiting up.

When I came in the door, I hugged them and told them. They started crying, and I cried along with them.

"But there's something I know Grandpa would want us to do." They looked up at me quizzically. "Eat ice cream."

So that's what we did. We sat on the couch and ate ice cream together. And cried.

KNOWING WHAT I KNOW NOW

I used to have a hard time showing my kids my worries. I thought if they saw me cry or worry, they'd think I was weak, and they wouldn't feel safe. I couldn't always hide my emotions from them, but I always felt guilty if they noticed—and especially if they helped me.

But then two things happened: I saw some movie that changed my mind. And I lost my dad and had so many tears I could no longer hide them. I started being more vulnerable in front of them. I'm so glad I did.

Don't be afraid to show your children your grief. Don't be afraid to break down and cry in front of them. Because here's one thing about parenting: if you try to suck it up and be the strong one, then they will think they're not allowed to be "weak" too. Cry in front of them. Lose your shit. Sit on the kitchen floor in your tears, and eat ice cream. Show them it's okay to have low times, then show them how to pick yourself up. I wish I would have had this realization when they were younger instead of always trying to be the "good mom."

Dad's funeral with folded flag

Chapter 10

CLOSURE

IT WASN'T SUPPOSED TO HAPPEN LIKE THIS.

I feel the need to say that again. It wasn't supposed to happen like this.

Dad and Max were supposed to live well into their eighties. Being the older brother, Dad would, of course, go first. He'd be hiking alone, and—distracted by a beautiful sunset over the Sierras—slip and fall right off the mountain. Max would simply fall asleep one night, after an incredible jam session with his buddies, and not wake up. For both, it'd be quick and painless.

It wasn't supposed to happen when they had so much life left in them, when they'd only had thirteen years to be brothers.

But when is life ever exactly what it's *supposed* to be?

Max's illness was so drawn out, so full of ups and downs, hopes and fears. Dad's was much quicker, and we really did think, right up to the end, that he would recover.

It's 2024 now. Max has been gone nineteen months and Dad one year. Adjusting to their dying within seven months of each other, following such different but terrible illnesses, has been tremendously difficult. I fell apart when Max died. I would wake up crying, and—so I wouldn't disturb my sleeping family—I would go downstairs and just cry on the couch. And not the *oh she cried herself to sleep*: it was the ugly, chest-heaving, can't-catch-your-breath crying.

Then, a short seven months later, when I hadn't even fully grieved the loss of Max yet, my dad went downhill and left me. I remember I just kept saying over and over, "This is bullshit!" I didn't take much time off work because I didn't know how to stay home alone and grieve. Looking back, I really should have taken a month off, maybe more. I should have used FMLA or something because I had a really rough time with my grief—anxiety, heightened blood pressure, weight gain, too much wine, and so on.

Eventually, with the help of Joe and my girls, my step-sister Alisha, and my good girlfriends, I was able to see the forest for the trees and started taking care of myself. I didn't want to ruin my health and put an expiration date on my own life. So as hard as it was, I stepped outside and took a walk. I cried on that walk a lot, sometimes not seeing the sidewalk in front of me through the tears. But after about a mile, I started looking around at the trees, the freshly mowed lawns, the blooming bushes, the young kestrels flying nearby in the blue sky, and I looked up and smiled. I felt like Dad was taking a walk with me—his leg issues gone and no need for a cane. But I still imagined I was holding his hand as I walked.

That was my start. One foot in front of the other, and before I knew it, I had walked three miles and was smiling. I was still sad and completely heartbroken, but I was smiling and feeling a sense of freshness, a sense of renewal, I guess. I made a plan to start getting back to my health. After all, my big five-oh birthday was coming up in a few months, and I did not want to look my age! It wasn't a perfect journey, but very very slowly I changed my bad habits, took the setbacks here and there, and mostly pushed forward, giving myself grace when I was sad and trying not to feel guilty when something made me happy.

I still talk to my dad a lot, especially when I'm in the car alone. Full-on conversations too. I tell him about my day, about how I went to our favorite salad place, and how I can see Grandma Gini's hill every day when I come to work.

* * *

As long as I can remember, Dad told me he wanted his ashes to be spread up on Grandma Gini's hill over Walnut Creek. He must have told me a million times.

We'd be driving through the area—often when he'd pick me up from work for us to go to lunch together—and he'd pull the car over.

"There's Grandma Gini's hill," he'd say, pointing up through the windshield.

"Yes, Dad. I know, you want your ashes there." I responded to him like this because we'd had that conversation more than two dozen times.

"It's important."

"Yeah, I know it's important," I said with a heartfelt tone.

"How will you do it?"

"I'll just walk up there and do it."

That always seemed to satisfy him, and we'd be back on our way.

It'd been many years since Grandma Gini lived there, but now the time had come. After not being able to fully honor my promise to keep him on the ventilator for three days, I felt even more compelled to honor this promise.

But when I imagined *just walking up there and doing it,* I grew apprehensive. I knew there was a particular area—an easement between properties—that wasn't *technically* on anyone's land, but I'd also have to do it during the daytime. What if someone saw me? Should I wear a disguise? And what would that even be? Camouflage? Not sketchy at all. Or maybe I should hide in plain sight—the bright orange of an electrical worker?

Ultimately, I decided to just risk it. So, a year after Dad passed, I brought tennis shoes and a small tin with me to work. Inside the tin was about a cup's worth of his ashes. I had other plans for the remainder of them.

On my lunch break, I changed shoes and took off for Grandma Gini's hill, which was quite close to my office building. Before I headed for the steep incline, though, I stopped at a florist to purchase a single sunflower, Dad's favorite. I then headed up a path that wound through the property at the back of Grandma Gini's, nervously patting the tin in my jacket pocket to make sure it was still there. A couple named Clyde and Josephine used to live on the land below, and Grandma Gini and I would cut through their yard if we were walking into town as a shortcut down the hill, often on our way to Genova's Deli so I could get my pickle.

I hoped no one was home. I didn't see any cars, at least.

When I reached the easement, I quickly and quietly found a spot I thought Dad would have liked. A patch of muddy ground underneath a walnut tree. The earthy smells transported me back to my childhood and afternoons with Grandma Gini.

I took out the tin, unscrewed the lid, and carefully scattered the ashes. I placed the sunflower on the ground. As if on cue and signifying the moment—like the toll of a church bell—a BART train whizzed by below.

A sob caught in my throat. I missed him beyond all measure.

But as I stood up and looked out over the hills and Mount Diablo, which was glowing green now, I could almost hear Dad saying, *Okay, my beautiful daughter.*

* * *

That summer, Joe and I went camping in Yosemite.

We stayed at the Wawona Campgrounds, only two sites away from Dad's favorite go-to site. I had brought more of Dad's ashes with me in a biodegradable scattering tube I had purchased on Amazon. It was decorated with a forest scene, perfect for the task at hand. For the next few days, Joe and I hiked around the area, making a point to stop in all of Dad's frequent haunts.

On top of Glacier Point. Along the Mist Trail by the waterfalls. In the Merced River at Indian Rock. Beside the old Horner cabin, where Dad had spent so many days as a child. And everywhere we went, I left some of him behind. I loved that he was now part of the land and the rocks and the water that he loved so dearly.

He was nearly home at last.

* * *

The only place left on my list is Big Meadow Lake outside of Spokane: that beautiful lake surrounded by pine forest, where Dad and Max loved to go fishing.

After Max lost his legs, Valerie's brother, Gregg, offered to take him out on his fishing boat, wheelchair and all. Max was thrilled, but they never got the chance. At Max's funeral, Gregg told my dad, "I still owe Max that fishing trip. It would be nice, Day, if you would come with me—and we'll have a chair open for Max." But, of course, they never got the chance either.

In the next year, I want to bring Dad's remaining ashes up to Big Meadow Lake. I think I'll ask Gregg if he's available to take me out on his fishing boat. I've kept Dad's rods and tackle. Maybe we'll bring a picnic, do a little fishing, and then scatter the ashes on the lake.

I like the poetry in this final act. I like that his remaining ashes will find their home in that lake, where he spent so many happy hours with his brother. A brother he never shared a home with as a child but with whom he shared a deep and beautiful bond. I like that those ashes will become a part of that lake, the mud, the fish, *the life* of it all.

* * *

When the last of Dad has been laid to rest, I expect I'll feel a sense of closure. In many ways, I haven't been able to fully accept the reality of his death. The past year has just been numb. I would ugly-cry out my grief for sure in the beginning, but as time goes on, it's grown less intense. There is still an underlying sadness that just never goes away. I used to feel like I was whole. Now I feel like a quarter of me has been taken away. Now I feel like I'm 75 percent of myself. I don't know if that will change or not, but that's how I feel now. That's the best way I can describe it.

I never knew what it was like to lose a parent. Even when Joe lost both his parents, I could feel it *with him*, but I never really knew what it was like. Until it happens to you, you never know how much it rips your heart out.

Once the burial ritual is complete, I think I'll begin to accept it.

But, at the same time, there's a chance that I'll never have closure about our family. Finding Max was an extraordinary blessing. For thirteen years, he added riches to all our lives. He gave my dad a bond of brotherhood that he'd never known was possible, and he gave me a beloved uncle. And the joy I feel, the profound sense of accomplishment I feel for having put the two of them together—despite all the locked doors and years of frustrating research—can't be underestimated. And yet, even after all this, I still have a lot of unanswered questions.

My original search, my original *drive*, was to uncover ancestral information. I've still never seen the original birth certificate. I still don't really know the full story of my grandmother, Virginia Whitley. And I yearn to know—perhaps even more so now that my dad is gone. Before it was all business, and I wanted to resolve it. But he wasn't supposed to die. I assumed I'd have it all wrapped up before he died. Not that there was a timeline, but I must have had an internal one I didn't know about. Now it's weighing on me to resolve it.

So once again I am petitioning the courts to open the adoption file and allow me access to the unamended birth certificate.

Naturally, nothing is online, even now. I mailed my petition to Sacramento—the original court that had sent me the non-identifying information. I dropped my package in the mail—making sure I had the right postage and a self-addressed, stamped envelope for their return response. Sheesh.

The first time I petitioned the courts, back in 1998, I believe I made the mistake of not having a thoughtful or thorough answer as to my cause for petitioning. I only said that I wished to know the information. But now, twenty-five years later, I was ready. I explained that every single person associated with this adoption from seventy-five years ago—mother, father, and son—was now dead. I have no siblings. No one would be harmed by the original birth certificate. Worried they would deny me the information since I wasn't the adoptee, I included Dad's death certificate that showed I was his only living relative. I also included documents to prove that I was not only the sole trustee of his entire estate but that I had durable power of attorney. As a final incentive, I reminded the Sacramento courts that an assembly bill in California that allows adoptees to access their birth certificates was currently being drafted.[4] And ten states allowed it already. I pleaded with them the best way I knew how and provided all of the evidence I could think of.

I didn't have to wait by the mailbox for long. Sacramento soon wrote back that I needed to petition the court in the county where the adoption had taken place. Brother. There went my tunnel vision, yet again. Dad's birth certificate says Santa Clara County, but the notes from Grandma Gini say San Francisco county. But, I thought, at least Sacramento looked! Maybe they were going to open it for me. Or maybe I'd just face yet another locked door.

So I repeated the process and sent my packet off to Santa Clara.

* * *

What a journey.

From the time I was a teenager in the late eighties to the young woman starting a search in the early nineties to the passion that enveloped a good part of my life until now as I approach my own second half of life. All the people I've met and connected with on this journey have been 99.9 percent positive. The Whitley cousins, Bonnie and Ernestine, who so graciously opened up

---

[4] CA Assembly Bill #1302: "This bill would, beginning January 1, 2025, require a superior court to grant a petition and require the State Registrar to provide a copy of the original unredacted birth certificate of an adopted person upon receipt of a verified petition filed by that adopted person who is 18 years of age or older and was the subject of an adoption occurring before January 1, 2025."

However, a brand new California Senate Bill 1274 was just introduced in early 2024. This bill would authorize disclosure of an original birth certificate, as defined, to an adopted person, or child or grandchild of an adopted person: "Notwithstanding any other provision of law, the State Registrar shall provide to an adopted person who is 18 years of age or older and who was born in this state, or to a direct line descendant of a deceased adopted person, a copy of the adopted person's original birth certificate, as defined in Section 102620, previously filed with the State Registrar."

their hearts and shared with me their photo albums and family stories, are priceless. Max, Valerie, Steven, Tania, and Ricardo became immediate family.

I wanted the mystery of my dad's adoption to be complete. But what I didn't realize was that I was actually searching for *my family* to be complete. Finding Max felt like a completion. And one my dad and I never knew we needed until we found it.

Learning about so many lies and hidden stories and finding so many locked doors has opened up my mind and changed the way I research. Because I discovered, again and again, that—like a true scientific researcher—my initial discoveries were not always the *absolute* truth, I now try not to take anything at face value or believe everything I hear or find online. I always, always try to dig a little deeper. I always corroborate my initial findings.

Doing genealogy and ancestry research my whole life, as a hobby for the most part, has definitely shaped the person I have become. Admittedly, it's probably made me a tad cynical, but I do think that's helped me down the line too.

The journey has also taught me the many different ways that a family can feel whole. With so many broken branches in my own family tree, my drive to uncover my dad's family secrets has been fueled by my need to keep my branch sturdy and intact.

I sincerely hope you, dear reader, have found inspiration in my journey. Whatever you do, never settle for locked doors. Keep searching for the right keys. They're out there. You just never know what feelings of wholeness may await you.

Grandma Gini's hill with Dad's sunflower

EPILOGUE

BEFORE MAX OR MY DAD DIED, A *SUPER CLOSE DNA match* with someone showed up on both my dad's and my profile on 23andMe.

This match did not overlap, though, with Max's profile. The only possible explanation for this was that the genetic connection must come from the birth father side, not from the Virginia Whitley side. This person, named Lisa, has a 4.36 percent DNA match to my dad and a 2.65 percent DNA match to me. These percentages might sound small, but they actually indicate a strong match.

Here's why:

My father shows up as roughly a 50 percent match with me because I received half of my DNA from him and half from my mother. One of my daughters, who also did the test, shows up as a 50 percent match to me. My half sister, Becky, with whom I share a mother, shows up as a 23 percent match. Uncle Max, whose mother is my paternal grandmother, shows up as a 10 percent match.

For my dad, his closest DNA matches rank, from highest to lowest percentages as me, Max, his granddaughter, and then this Lisa. After that, his matches are second, third, and distant cousins. 23andMe actually categorizes a 4.36 percent match as a *first cousin*. This doesn't necessarily mean it's a "cousin" in the true sense, but that's how the software categorizes it.

As soon as I saw this match appear on the site, I clicked on Lisa's profile. Get this: in her list of family surnames, she includes a J—, an F—, and *Corsaw*.[5]

Remember the Corsaws? The foster family who Virginia Whitley went to live with when her mother, Bessie, died? Yep, those Corsaws. Not exactly a common name. In fact, according to Forebears.io, Corsaw is actually the 2,091,648th most frequent surname on earth. I immediately begin questioning Virginia's time with the family. Did she have relations with somebody in the Corsaw household? Was she sexually assaulted?

I then hopped on over to Ancestry.com. You may recall that in 2009, after our first visit to Texas, I corresponded with Sandra Corsaw, the granddaughter of Harry and Hazel Corsaw, who fostered Virginia. Afterward, I began building a Corsaw family tree on Ancestry.com.

And guess what I discovered. Sandra Corsaw does indeed have a daughter named Lisa! Not only that, but she is also connected to the surnames J— and F—.

Oh my God, I thought. *My father is somehow related to Sandra Corsaw.* So much for my idea that Virginia had a fling with a cook in the Navy. So much for the court-provided non-identifying information that Virginia listed about a so-called birth father. All of it was obviously lies to cover up something that happened

---

5 Full omitted for privacy.

while she was in foster care. My mind was blown. I was freaking out with this new information.

Should I call my dad? No, I immediately thought. *How horrible would it be to find out that your birth was a result of sexual assault?*

So I called Max and Valerie instead and told them everything. They, too, were dumbfounded by the information.

Finally, Max said, "You know, a memory just popped into my head from my childhood. We were at an outdoor event—my parents were visiting with some friends, sitting at picnic tables, and all the kids were running around and playing. And you know how you remember kind of listening to the adult conversations but not really paying attention? Well, I remember my mom saying to the adults around the table, 'He raped me.' I didn't know what the word rape meant, so didn't think anything of it and went on playing. I haven't recalled that memory in *years*."

Valerie and I were shocked at this revelation. *Max* was shocked at this revelation.

Then Max said, "You can't tell your dad."

"Yeah, I was wondering about that," I said. "That's why I called you all first."

"He doesn't want to know any of this, Jennifer. Please don't tell him."

I trusted Max wholeheartedly and promised not to tell my dad. And I never did. He died not knowing anything about his birth father.

I'm sad to think that my dad could have been the product of rape, but I really don't know for sure and probably never will. But I'm glad that Virginia Whitley chose the path she did and gave my dad up for adoption to a good family to raise him without that stigma hovering over him his whole life.

In the past couple of years, though, I did attempt to reach out to Lisa on 23andMe as well as Ancestry.com through their messenger features. She responded at one point, but I didn't see it right away. When I finally did, she had sent a second message saying not to bother her or her family, and she blocked me on Ancestry.com from seeing her profile or messaging her.

I also wrote to Sandra a few times within the last couple of years, trying to gently explain my DNA findings, but she wrote back that she didn't know what I was talking about and she couldn't help me. I imagine that the thought of her father or grandfather possibly having had a secret child with Virginia Whitley was a bit much to take in and could really upset her apple cart.

So I'm letting it go.

I'm very sad about this, as it is one more locked door. I desperately want to keep writing to Sandra and make her see my point of view, but it's just not the right thing to do, no matter how much I want to wrap up the entire search in one neat box with a bow on top. I just can't keep hounding them.

And I do, of course, have empathy for Lisa's and Sandra's situation. I was extremely lucky and blessed that Max was so accepting of finding he had a brother he never knew about. And I guess I cannot expect the same from everyone. Sandra could be my dad's sister, and Lisa could be my cousin! Regardless, at this point, there's nothing more I can do that would be morally responsible.

I hold out hope that someday this book makes it to Sandra and her daughters and they reach out to me to make a connection. I would really like to see photos of Lyle, Harry, and Sandra and see if my dad resembles any of them.

I also hope that my petitions to the Santa Clara courts will prove fruitful. But I'm also prepared that Virginia lied or left further information about the father blank—and that I'll never know.

MISCELLANEOUS PHOTOGRAPHS

Max, Annabelle, and Valerie

Dad climbing Half Dome

Dad being silly with me at the Bay to Breakers in San Francisco

Father–daughter dance at Dad's surprise sixtieth birthday party

Cousins Tania and Steven

MISCELLANEOUS PHOTOGRAPHS · 175

Max and Valerie wedding photo circa 1974

Dad and mom's wedding, 1972, with Grandma Gini and Lyle

Dad being silly at Easter

Dad's folded flag and his Marine medals earned in Vietnam

"Gio Linh"
September 67

Dad on his 88" Howitzer named "Wild Thing" in Vietnam circa 1967

Early Years

On the "hill" in Walnut Creek

Viet Nam

Birthday cake his mom shipped to him. He often shared fond memories about her.

  He carried on from his grarage band days in high school with his guitar. Stayed in touch with his military buddies and often went to reunions. Favorite band was the Eagles. He finally got to see them in person a couple years ago.

Life in the Foothills

"He's a handful, but we love him!" - Jim English

- Loved to fish and visit with his many friends.
. . . *"Day, do you have your hearing aids in?"*

"Day-o" loved popcorn, pizza, & apple pie!

Claimed he hated dogs, then would go over and pet them.

His tan body
calves hard as rocks
eyes squinting towards the sun.
His Granite face, Old
Historic.
8,000 feet, 16 hours
22 pounds
Grab the left over
gloves, left before.
Am I ready?
Can I do this?
Perspiration, anticipation.
Carabineer attached. Take
a deep breath. Take
the first leap.
Biceps burning, pulling
cables ringing
vibrations unsteady.
Push further. Doubt
creeps in. Arguing.
Faith pulls out.
Eyes searching, horizon
rising, shorter, shorter.
Panting. Quads contract
at last the giant step
Up! 64 years.
The Gray Conqueror!

By Jennifer Wallig   July 2012

The
World
Famous
Talking
Bear
Oakhurst, CA
2010

2018

Life is Good

Until We Meet Again...

Loved His Family

Thanks to Jennifer's research, Day was united with the half-brother he did not know he had. He would visit out of state with Max, Valerie, and family on a regular basis.

Bay to Breakers   60th Birthday Party   Daddy's Girl

Dayz Place

Excerpts from Dad's funeral program

Steve, Grandma Gini, and Dad at the house in Walnut Creek

Virginia Whitley's Bible College photo, signed to the Corsaws

Virginia Whitley a few months after giving birth to my dad, in front of "Corsaw" real estate office where she worked

Virginia Whitley later in life, circa 1980s

Grandma Gini's high school grad photo

Memorial Service of

Wilford Max Frazier

Sat. Nov. 12th, 2022 at 2:00pm

Nov. 3rd 1953 — Oct. 2nd 2022

Max, Valerie, Tania & Steven

1990

In addition to music, Max also loved hunting and fishing!

Max & Valerie, with grandkids Miah, Kaelyn, Elisha & Gabriel.

A note sent to Valerie from one of the nurses after Max's passing:

"Valerie, it broke my heart to hear about Max's passing. His witness touched so many lives in our department as we cared for him and he will be missed. I have no doubt that we will see him again in heaven. He truly "fought the good fight.""

A vision Gabriel (Max's grandson) had about three weeks before Max's passing:

" I saw Grandpa dancing with his new legs in heaven with a look of contentment on his face, as well as pure joy. This wasn't just dancing though, it was twirling as well as flipping, and jumping in the air. He had all his agility back, no more bad back, no more bad heart, none of it. It also was an act of worship as well, I couldn't tell you why I knew, I just knew. He was doing what he loved best in the most fitting way possible."

-II Timothy 4:7-8

" I have fought the good fight, I have finished the race, I have kept the faith. Finally, there is laid up for me the crown of righteousness, which the Lord, the righteous Judge, will give to me on that day, and not to me only but also to all who have loved His appearing."

Max's funeral program

Lyle and me

Dad fishing

Max fishing

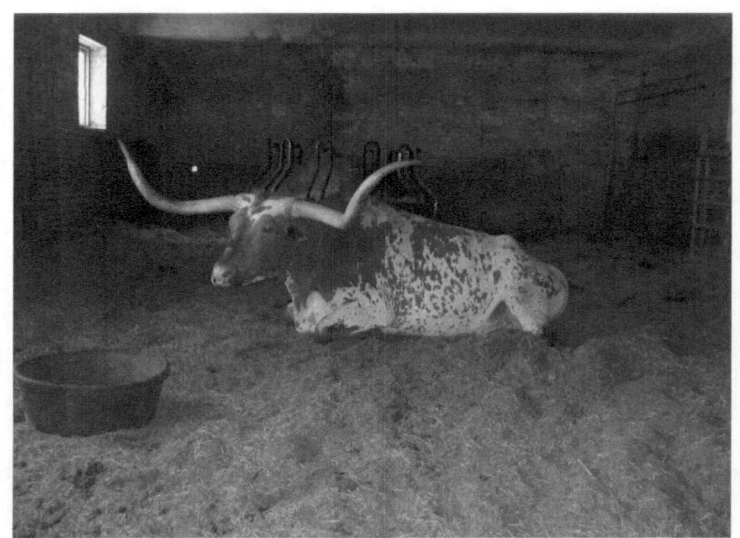

A Texas Longhorn from when we visited the Stockyards in Fort Worth

♀ PROGRESS...

IT RAINED ALL NIGHT IN STOCKTON
AND MY SLEEPING BAG GOT SOAKED,
I WOKE UP THIS MORNING
I WAS COLD, WET AND BROKE,
SO I LIT UP MY LAST PIPE LOAD
AT THE SACRAMENTO COUNTY LINE CUZ,
I'VE GOT RECOVERY ON MY MIND.

I LOVED THAT RED EYE WHISKY
AND KNOWN TO DRINK BEER TOO,
STAYING UP LATE HIGH ON SPEED
WHAT'S AN ADDICT TO DO,
I KNOW THAT THERE'S A GOD
AND HE'S FORGIVING, LOVING AND KIND CUZ,
I'VE GOT RECOVERY ON MY MIND.

SO I CHECKED INTO A REHAB HOUSE
IN MAY OF 95,
I ADMITTED THAT I WAS POWERLESS
AND BEGAN TO SEE THE LIGHT,
EASY DOES IT THEY SAID BUT DO IT
ONE DAY AT A TIME CUZ,
I'VE GOT RECOVERY ON MY MIND.

HAVING WORKED THE STEPS WITH A SPONSOR
FROM MY MIND DOWN TO MY HEART,
MY MIND GETS ME IN TROUBLE
AND I REFUSE TO GET TOO SMART,
ACCEPT THE THINGS I CAN NOT CHANGE
AND CHANGE THE THINGS I CAN CUZ,
RECOVERY HAS MADE ME A BRAND NEW MAN.

CONTINUING TO WORK MY PROGRAM
AND GIVING AWAY THESE THINGS I HAVE,
BY NO MEANS WELL AND WONDERFUL
BUT MUCH MORE THAN I HAD,
STEP BY STEP AND DAY BY DAY
IT'S GETTING BETTER ALL THE TIME CUZ,
RECOVERY IS IN MY HEART NOT JUST MY MIND.

KEEP COMING BACK IT WORKS IF YOU WORK IT
THIS IS WHAT THEY SAY,
BE OF SERVICE AND GET INVOLVED
AND DON'T FORGET TO PRAY,
Uncover, Discover and Discard
And be sure to clean house Too Cuz,
A clean Life The New Millennium
has for you!

DAY H.

Dad's poem about recovery

Dad's fifteen years of sobriety chips

Spreading ashes in Yosemite: covered bridge

Indian Rock

Swinging bridge

Tunnel view

ADDITIONAL RESOURCES

I HAVE INCLUDED SOME ORGANIZATIONS AND WEBsites below that are quite helpful.

RESOURCES FOR GENEALOGY, DNA, AND SEARCHING
- International Soundex Reunion Registryisrr.org/
- ALMA Society legacy facebook page facebook.com/groups/1093445390976 11
- PACER acebook.com/pacerinfo
- Social Security Death Index familysearch.org/search/collection/1202535
- 23andme
- adoption.com/
- adopted.com/
- Bastard Nation—bastards.org/
- findmyfamily.org/
- familysearch.org/en/united-states/
- ancestry.com

- searchangels.org/
- adopteerightslaw.com/

RESOURCES FOR SOBRIETY (AA AND NA)

- progresshouseinc.org/ The Progress House is where my dad got sober
- aa.org/
- na.org/

RESOURCES FOR VETERANS

- va.gov/
- calvet.ca.gov/calvet-programs/veteran-services
- To connect with a **Veterans Crisis Line** responder anytime day or night:
    - Dial 988 then Press 1.
    - Start a confidential chat.
    - Text 838255.
    - If you have hearing loss, call TTY: 800-799-4889.

ADOPTION LAW ADVOCACY

- You will need to find your own legislature so you can tell them how you feel about the restrictions imposed on adult adoptees and how they violate your civil rights by barring you from knowing about your own truth.
    - house.gov/representatives/find-your-representative
    - congress.gov/members/find-your-member
- In California: findyourrep.legislature.ca.gov/
    - SB 1274: legiscan.com/CA/bill/SB1274/2023
    - AB 1302: legiscan.com/CA/text/AB1302/id/2750692

ACKNOWLEDGMENTS

THIS BOOK HAS BEEN A JOURNEY THAT ILLUSTRATES my lifelong quest to find answers. There are so many people who have been an inspiration to me along the way that I couldn't possibly name them all. The heartfelt encouragement has been appreciated more than I can express. Thank you for helping me and I hope you know who you are.

Thank you to Mela for being my surrogate therapist for almost a year and helping me get the words out.

Thank you to Sarah for being my "lookout" on that Walnut Creek hill.

Thank you to my out-of-state besties who listened to me cry and gave me advice to conquer my roadblocks.

Thank you to my soul sister, Alisha, for countless hours of listening to me second-guess my direction and constantly putting me back on track.

To my daughters, who are some of the strongest, smartest, and unconditionally loving women I know: thank you for being good to your mom. I love you kiddos.

And to my most awesome husband, who I couldn't do this life without: thank you for always having the most down-to-earth and no-nonsense perspectives, and thank you for being my life partner. I love you mucho.

But Ruth replied,

"Don't urge me to leave you or to turn back from you. Where you go I will go, and where you stay I will stay. Your people will be my people and your God my God."

—RUTH 1:16

ABOUT THE AUTHOR

—

JENNIFER WALLIG has been passionate about ancestry and genealogy for as long as she can remember.

When she began her search for her father's birth family, she had no access to the internet or to any of today's helpful technology. Today, though, with a plethora of information on her side—including private databases and newspaper archives—the sky's the limit! She started Blurred Lines Genealogy, dedicated to helping others solve their own ancestry mysteries. In addition to her father's family, she's discovered additional ancestors—including a connection to Laura Ingalls Wilder and an accused Salem witch. You can reach out to her at blurredlinesgeni@gmail.com for more information on how she might help you clear up your blurred lines.

A native Northern Californian, Jennifer loves spending time in nature with her husband and two daughters. Yosemite National Park is one of their favorite places to hike and camp. She also enjoys bike rides, crocheting, and backyard barbeques.

www.ingramcontent.com/pod-product-compliance
Lightning Source LLC
Chambersburg PA
CBHW030520080526
44586CB00011B/263